FOUNDATIONS OF FUTUROLOGY IN EDUCATION

Edited by

Richard W. Hostrop

An ETC Publication
1973

C I P

Library of Congress Cataloging in Publication Data

Hostrop, Richard W.
  Foundations of futurology in education.
  (Education futures, no. 1)
    1. Educational planning.   2. Forecasting.
  I. Title
LA 131.H75   371.2'07   73-6855
ISBN 0-088280-006-X $7.95

Copyright © 1973 by ETC PUBLICATIONS
                    Palm Springs
                    California 92262

CONTENTS

452240

FOREWORD

FOUNDATIONS OF FUTUROLOGY IN EDUCATION is the first in a series of works to be published by ETC concerned with the future of education. This first work's purpose is to introduce to educational practitioners and future educational practitioners alike the thinking of futurologists (or futurists) — particularly as related to futurology (or futuristics) of the Great Social Enterprise: Education. But FOUNDATIONS OF FUTUROLOGY IN EDUCATION has been prepared with a still larger view in mind. The *significance* of futurists's thinking to education is also illuminated. Moreover, the reader is introduced to some of the primary tools of futurists, along with ample illustrations as to how they can be used to improve the educational enterprise. Finally, the user of this anthology is taken on an exhilarating mental adventure by ingesting conceptual views of the future as presented by leading futurists.

FOUNDATIONS OF FUTUROLOGY IN EDUCATION provides the reader with a comprehensive introduction to a serious new discipline by futurologists of international first rank. This work is intended as an early step in the direction of reversing Alvin Toffler's observation: ". . . our schools face backward toward a dying system, rather than forward to the emerging new society . . . people tooled for survival in a system that will be dead before they are." To aid in reversing Toffler's observed dire trend, the future must be studied *at least* as seriously as the past is studied. We must become future oriented if for no other reason than it is the *only* way of even having a chance of staying even with the geometric explosion of knowledge and changing socioeconomic conditions. If we do not *plan,* we can only flouderingly *react* to events after they have passed. It is the intention of this work, and others to follow in the series on the future of education, to aid in the crucial imperative upon us — to *plan* and *lead* as well as to effectively *administer* the educational enterprises.

Homewood, Illinois   Richard W. Hostrop

Part I

INTRODUCING THE FUTURE

Today we increasingly believe that there is conscious discipline —
already learnable though perhaps not yet teachable —
for the imaginative leap into the unknown.
We are developing rigorous methods for creative perception.
Unlike the science of yesterday,
it is not based on organizing our knowledge.
It is based on organizing our ignorance.

PETER DRUCKER

"Landmarks of Tomorrow"

Toffler: Learning to Live With Future Shock

Alvin Toffler

TODAY SOCIETY NEEDS AN EDUCATIONAL
APPROACH THAT IS THE ANTITHESIS OF THE
ONE DEVELOPED FOR INDUSTRIALISM, AND
THE YOUNG PEOPLE ARE SOMEHOW ALMOST
INSTINCTIVELY AWARE OF THIS.

College and University Business: In your best sel-
ler, "Future Shock, " you say that advanced technological societies such as ours are rushing headlong
into a socioeconomic condition that you call super-
industrialism. By not adjusting to this new condition
we are in danger of incurring mass future shock.
Would you explain what is super-industrialism and
how it leads to future shock, as well as what are the
characteristics of future shock?

Toffler: Jean Fourastie, the French planner and
social philosopher, has declared that, "Nothing will
be less industrial than the civilization born of the
Industrial Revolution. " By super-industrialism I
do not mean to imply a mere super-extension of
industrialism, a bigger, better industrialism. I
am speaking of a radical break from industrialism
as radical as the automobile was from the horse-
drawn carriage.

Super-industrialism is based principally on technological change. Before industrialism goods

Reprinted with permission from the September, 1971
College and University Business.Copyright 1971,
McGraw-Hill Pubs., Inc., Chicago.

were hand produced. They required individual work and attention, and production was custom production. Whether it was a pair of boots, a chain of mail, earthenware utensils, they were made one at a time. Super-industrialism is based on almost a dialectic return to what might be called not handcraft but headcraft. Production is based on a fusion of mass production and custom production. An example: In the traditional clothing factory, many layers of cloth are placed on top one another and a worker with a knife cuts the outline of the suit before the suit is made. The pressure is always to find a more powerful knife so that he can cut more layers of suit into identical patterns. That's the pressure of mass production. However, in super-industrialism we now have a computer-operated laser gun that doesn't cut 10 suits or 100 suits or 1,000 suits, but it cuts one suit at a time. It is programmed to cut one suit at a time and yet it does it faster and cheaper than the old way of mechanically cutting many suits at a time. This same analogous trend is happening in many industries. This is a fundamental change in the technological system of industrialism.

It not only means that soon many machines will be synchronized to the billionth of a second, but that man can and must start to de-synchronize. It means that the sameness, the conformity of goods and services of the industrial age, can explode into a diversity of choice with which man could have great difficulty in coping. It portends the breakdown of the hierarchically bureaucratic system of management of the industrial age: With the acceleration in the production of goods and services, there needs be a corresponding acceleration in the decision making process.

Future shock is a word I coined a few years back to describe the distress, both physical and psychological, that arises from an overload of the human organism's physical adaptive systems and its decision making processes. It is the human response to overstimulation. The human organism has limits to the amount of change it can absorb. Different people react to future shock in different ways. Its symptoms also vary according to the stage and intensity of the disease. These symptoms range all the way from anxiety, hostility to helpful authority and seemingly senseless violence, to physical illness, depression and apathy. Its victims often manifest erratic swings in interest and life style, followed by an effort to 'crawl into their shells' through social, intellectual and emotional withdrawal. They feel continually bugged or harassed, and want desperately to reduce the number of decisions they must make. Uncontrolled, unmanaged, super-industrialism could lead to mass future shock.

C & UB: In "Future Shock" you say that the prime objective for education in the super-industrial age must be to increase the individual's cope-ability, the speed and economy with which he can adapt to continual change. Isn't that what our educational system is attempting to do now?

Toffler: No. Absolutely not, in almost every case. What passes for education today, even in our 'best' schools and colleges, is a hopeless anachronism. Government ministries, churches, the mass media-- all exhort young people to stay in school, insisting that now, as never before, one's future is almost wholly dependent upon education. Yet for all this rhetoric about the future, our schools face backward toward a dying system. Their vast energies are applied to cranking out industrial man.

It was for this reason that education, in its very structure, simulated industrialism. The most criticized features of education today--the regimentation, lack of individualization, the rigid systems of seating, groupings, grading and marking, the authoritarian role of the teacher--are precisely those that made mass public education so effective an instrument of adaptation for its place and time.

Today society needs an educational approach that is the antithesis of the one developed for industrialism, and the young people are somehow almost instinctively aware of this. The difficulty is that those in charge of the institutions were raised in the industrial age and still think there is value in producing industrial men.

C & UB: What advice would you give to a president of a college to prepare his school for the next 25 years, for producing individuals who could cope in super-industrialism?

Toffler: First, I would have him organize his administrative structure, which is probably based on industrial bureaucracy, toward adhocratic forms of organization. In an accelerated society where transient problems, opportunities and relationships will be commonplace, slow, methodical organizations cannot cope. The milelong lines of students at registration time, the red tape in attempting to change a course or a school, the ability of a school to take advantage of grants or forestall fiscal crises all this demands an organization from which information can be obtained quickly. Groups of experts can

be rallied together just as quickly to make judgment
on it, and competent decisions are made at the lowest
most accessible "level" of the administration.

Second, I would have him examine closely his admissions criteria. The obsession with SAT scores and
grades has been revealed to be grotesque. Anybody
who still operates on that basis is ultimately writing
a death warrant for his institution. Third, he should
call his students together, along with the faculty and
his administration, and ask them to suggest what the
goals of the institution should be in five to 10 years.

The fourth thing he should do is to re-examine the
relationship between his institution and the local
community. He should find out what are the problems
in the community dealing with those problems. Finally, he should re-examine the faculty's relationship
to the school, recognizing that faculties are frequently the most conservative elements in the entire university system. In this connection, I would take on
two issues: one is tenure and the other, a redefini-
tion of the word "professor."

The existing college and university instructional
structure has not even reached the level of industrial
bureaucracy; it's unadulterated feudalism. Even the
word tenure goes back to feudalistic land tenure. The
departmental principalities are dominated by senior
faculty barons to the exclusion of the young serfs who
teach in the department. The problem is how to re-
distribute these resources when up against built-in
rigidities.

As for redefining the word professor, I would like to
say out loud what everybody knows and that is that

there are frequently people in the community who have skills, knowledge, insight and wisdom to impart that far exceeds anything that the faculty has. These people are in touch with change, they face pressures that faculty people do not because of the artificial situation of the university. A concrete example of how these off-campus expertises can be used: Ever since I was seven years old, I knew I wanted to be a writer. Despite the fact that I was educated in New York, which is the national headquarters of publishing, journalism, public relations, and advertising, I went through 20 years of my life without ever meeting a person who made a living using words. Now that's criminally insane.

C & UB: Are you optimistic about the future of higher education?

Toffler: The universities and colleges are in for a difficult time. Part of the immediate problem is the ideological retrenchment in education that is being justified by the Nixon recession, along with the general fiscal crunch that higher education is caught in. Many of your better futuristic educators, who necessarily do not 'fit' into the industrial mold of education, are being laid off. This is resulting in concentrated conservative educational systems that are nonfunctional. The potential students retaliate by simply not attending the institution.

But from a broader perspective, there is a more profound reason that institutions of higher learning will suffer dearly during the next five or 10 years. This was recently impressed on me while rereading the five and 10 year old predictions made by sociologists like Daniel Bell. They claimed that we had entered

a post industrial period, and predicted that the universities were going to be the dominant institution
of that time: The age would flux around ideas and
the university is the natural repository of ideas. Na-
turally these were university-biased sociologists.
I, on the other hand, believe that we are moving into
super-industrialism and I doubt very seriously that
the university is going to be the pivotal institution
of that age. I think the future is going to be particularly difficult for the prestigious institutions, such
as Yale, Columbia and Stanford. These were successful during the industrial age and will find it aw-
fully difficult to adjust to super-industrialism for
that reason. In an accelerated time in which ideas
and values alter rapidly, stratified institutions will
not be able to change rapidly enough. Society,
therefore, will seek more creative and innovative
ways of educating people. I see industry taking a
hand here. Not only will it continue to have on-the-
job training, but I foresee it sponsoring living/learn-
ing communes. Presently there are living/learning
collaboratives that are based primarily on group dy-
namics and the search for better human relationships.
I would like to see experiments with learning communes that devote themselves to studying physics and
the social implications of physics, or that devote
themselves to biological revolution. Until now the
revolt against the university and the creation of experimental parrallel institutions has been one-sided.
The radicals who experiment with new forms have
turned their backs on technoligical society as a
whole, often in an excess of middle-class romanti-
cism. My own feeling is that this is beginning to
change, that there is a new generation of young
people who are not blindly anti-technological, who

see the possibilities for using video-cassettes, computer systems, lasers and the whole panoply of technology in more humane ways.

"Future Shock" has been a best-seller since first
issued in July 1970, making the condition and its
author, Alvin Toffler, household names. A news-
paperman, magazine writer, author of books, Mr.
Toffler is also a consultant to many of the world's
largest business corporations.

Theobald: Educating People for the Communications Era

Robert Theobald

THE EMERGENCE OF THE COMMUNICATIONS ERA
BASED ON FULL EDUCATION MEANS THE END OF
THE INDUSTRIAL ERA BASED ON FULL EMPLOY-
MENT. THE INDUSTRIAL ERA REQUIRED THAT
EVERYBODY TOIL; THE COMMUNICATIONS ERA
WILL ALLOW EVERYBODY A REASONABLE STAN-
DARD OF LIVING WITHOUT TOIL BUT WITH SELF-
CHOSEN WORK.

College and University Business: After reading your
various books and your speeches, it becomes clear
that the educational system you hope to achieve is dependent on major changes in what you choose to call
the idea-structures on which this country functions,
which in turn will not only bring about change in the
country's educational system but other social systems
as well as economic and political changes to the country.

Theobald: That's very true. We in this country are
in serious trouble principally because we are still
using outdated idea-structures: All our institutions,
including higher education, were designed to reinforce
these existing idea-structures. It follows, therefore,
that if we are to create and circulate new idea-structures, we shall need new institutions and new culture.

C & UB: In your speech before the American Society
of Newspaper Editors this year you said that it is not

Reprinted with permission from the September, 1971
College and University Business, Copyright 1971.
McGraw-Hill Pubs., Inc., Chicago.

possible to change a total system unless those involved comprehend a changed perception of the nature of the universe. Do new idea-structures come from this chang-ed perception as well as help to bring it about?

Theobald: Let me say it another way. The Industrial Age, which is now over, had two primary goals: to achieve the maximum rate of economic growth and to distribute the consequent production through full employment. Now these goals were based on unprovable assumptions: that it was best for man to achieve maximum rates of economic growth and that this material growth could best be distributed to people through full employment. To achieve these goals expeditiously, society created a view of man which would achieve these goals.

I believe psychologist B. F. Skinner of "Walden Two" fame adequately sums up the way society saw man during the Industrial Age, and the way most of our educational institutions still see their students. Man, Skinner says, is moved only by negative and positive sanctions--the whip and the carrot--and any meas-ures that tend to remove the threat of the whip and the promise of the carrot would contribute to the collapse of society. In education this idea-structure was perpetrated through grades, degrees, fear of being kicked out of school, of not being able to get a job without a degree, and more recently by the threat of being drafted and sent to Viet Nam.

C & UB: Is there an alternative way to see man?

Theobald: The late Abraham Maslow, the psycho-logist, has some appropriate insights on this. Maslow

theorizes that man has a hierarchy of needs and as
the more basic needs are satisfied, higher needs,
such as doing things that give people satisfaction,
achieve more importance. Through the single-mind-
edness of the Industrial Age, an affluence came
that allowed masses of succeeding generations to
seek higher ends than security, food, clothing and
shelter. But the difficulty was that society was not
adaptable to this almost new species of being. What
Maslow calls the self-actualized man. This is a
person, according to Maslow and from my own observation, who accepts himself, others and nature.
He has enough self-esteem and confidence to have no
need to tear others down. He has an uncommon absence of the fears, frustrations, and pressuring needs
which limit families, friends and acquaintances, and
other aspects of the external world.

C & UB: How did we get to our present situation?

Theobald: During the postwar years, we have been
achieving economic growth but we also have been
saying that this growth does not change the system.
It's a most extraordinary argument, when you get
right down to it. In other words, we can build more
highways, we can have more cars, more colleges,
more universities, but this growth will not make any
fundamental changes in the system. We have forgotten
that sufficient change in quantity always changes quality. Almost all of the well-known futurists are still
involved in this sort of thinking. For example, they
look at university growth over the next 25 years and
extend the curve, not recognizing that trends have
already changed. On a more sophisticated level people such as Herman Kahn, Daniel Bell, Alvin Toffler,
whom I call positive extrapolators, are trapped in

this linear type of thinking.

On the other side, you have what I call the negative extrapolators. These include the Students for Democratic Action, many ecologists, the Student Mobilization Committee. They believe that the future is determined in exactly the same way as do the positive extrapolators: that Western man has determined his future fate by his past decisions. However, they are so horrified by the direction in which these past decisions are taking us, that they are prepared to tear down the society to save us from the consequences of our past actions. They are attempting to create a neo-Luddite revolt. Just as Britons smashed machines in the early Nineteenth Century in an attempt to avoid change, so these Americans are trying to turn off technology and return to an earlier state. The defeat of the Supersonic Transport was partly owing to this type of thinking.

The positive and negative extrapolators both are saying that the trends in America can be expected to continue, that such changes in trend as occur will be minor, and that the world in the year 2000 will be a larger, flashier, but still recognizable version of the world in 1971. Toffler in "Future Shock" calls it Super-Industrialism.

And here I come back to the central point: To a great extent it has been our educational system that has made both the positive and negative extrapolators blind to any creative alternatives. Through education's reliance on deductive thinking, its fear of the creative, subjective and inductive thought processes, its demand that students merely regurgitate

what the professors and text books say, it has in-
grained people into thinking that they cannot handle
anything new. The only ideas that seem valid are
ones that are based on an extrapolation of the past.

C & UB: So far you have painted a rather bleak future. In " An Alternative Future for America II"
you speak optimistically about the fact that although
the Industrial Age is over, America has entered
into a new, exciting Communications Era.

Theobald: Yes, we have entered the Communications
Era but unless the majority of the people become
aware of it and act on that awareness this reality does
us very little good. Arnold Toynbee, the British historian, has pointed out that past cultures have found
it impossible to keep up with fundamental change in
the conditions in which they lived. People continued
to use data based on obsolete idea-structures and in
the process, destroyed their cultures. If we are to
survive we must somehow create a-historical patterns which permit us to change idea-structures.

Elizabeth Sewell said, when she was dean of Bensa-
lem College at Fordham University, that we don't
have to achieve change because the Industrial Era
institutions have already ceased to exist. This
sounds nonsensical but perhaps I can produce an
image which will make some sense of it. Let me
suggest to you that we live on a vast plain on which
there are a large number of castles. These castles
representing our institutions, are unguarded: The
moats are empty and the drawbridges are down. All
we have to do is walk into the castles--the old insti-
tutions--and take everything out of them that would

be valuable for the future. It is necessary to tiptoe in because there are some people who will get mad if you disturb them. Unfortunately, the negative extrapolators who have been trying to get change up to now haven't been satisfied to tiptoe in and take what they wanted. They have assembled outside the castle and blown their trumpets and claimed they were coming to take over. The defenders, in a last burst of energy, have slaughtered the attackers.

I believe the primary reason people have been unwilling to tiptoe in is their fundamental insecurity. In order for many people to know that they are doing good things they need to be convinced that somebody they dislike believes they were doing bad things.

C & UB: Then the first step to bring about change is a psychological one? It is to make people aware that they are, or can become, self-actualized and it is to give them enough assurance of this that they will not need to take issue with those who are irrelevant anyway? But how do you create the new institutions for this forthcoming Communications Era?

Theobald: Yes, you're quite right, the first step is psychological. At present, there are a number of groups attempting to bring this about. I am thinking of the Esalen Institutes, Human Potential Seminars, various encounter and T groups. In the future, I see our educational system serving this function.

Now as to the second point you raised: How do we create new institutions for the Communications Era? Let me first point out why the Industrial Era cannot continue. Our new knowledge of social and physical sciences shows that if systems are to survive they must ensure four things: accurate movement of information, decision making to ensure correction of divergencies from desired trends, prevention of growth beyond the capabilities of the system, and prevention of overload of decision-making capacity. Our present political, economic and societal systems, including almost every level of education, breaks every one of these systematic requirements. We justify inaccurate movement of information under three names: public relations, advertising and management of news. Through centralized government we prevent people from being more responsible. The ecology crisis has pointed out that we are not living within the size of our system: America should not be using 60 per cent or so of the world's natural resources. Finally, in terms of input and output, the hierarchical structure of our corporations, our universities, and our political institutions require that single individuals or small groups make decisions, when it is humanly impossible for them to be aware of all the relevant information.

C & UB: How will institutions of high learning function in the future Communications Era?

Theobald: Education will be a life long pursuit. Education will be considered the process of providing each individual with the capacity to develop his potential to the full. This requires that we enlarge the individual's perceptive ability by providing a sufficiently wide range of diversified societal environments so that the talent of all can be used. The emergence of the Communications Era based on full education means the end of the Industrial Era based on full employment. The Industrial Era re-

quired that everybody toil; the Communications Era
will allow everybody a reasonable standard of living
without toil but with self-chosen work.

Now to get back to your original question: How will
institutions of higher learning function in this future
community? I see only two means by which the universities and colleges will survive in the future. We
will perceive these better if we look first at why many
institutions are going to die in the Seventies. The most
obvious reason is that the financial crisis is much more
serious than anyone is willing to discuss. It will get
worse because large numbers of middle class parents
aren't going to be able to send their children to schools
as tuitions increase. Also increasing numbers of the
brightest kids are deciding that they can find their edu-
cations in a different way. I think a lot of other youngsters are only staying in college because there are few
options to do otherwise. But this is changing, partly
because people will not need a B.A. or a Ph.D. to get
a job, but also because society is opening up and there
are increasingly varied ways to live.

I can see only two ways in which the schools can get
out of this bind. The first way is for the university
to become the brains of the area in which it is located.
That means you bring in people to teach who live in
the area. The whole idea that the professor has to be
a full-time educator is ridiculous. How much better,
both economically for the institution and for the psychological growth of the students, to bring in engi-
neers, architects, lawyers, bankers and writers who
are living in the real world and who, therefore, have
to teach out of reality. The students also must become more integrated into the community. The stu-

dent body will not be limited to ages from 18 to 22.
The extraordinary distinction between education and
continuing education will be eliminated and the institution will melt back into the town.

The other thing a university can do if it wishes to
survive during the next 25 years is to begin to specialize like the University of Wisconsin at Green
Bay...to deal with a particular problem/possibility
center. Green Bay's emphasis is environment; a
variety of skills--sciences, social science, the arts
focus on that area.

C & UB: In traveling around the country and meeting
administrators generally are more receptive to change
and suggested alternatives in education than the faculty. Has this been your experience?

Theobald: Yes, faculty is more threatened by change
and for good reason. Teachers at the moment often
act as surrogate programed learning devices. They
move information which could be better moved by
film, by television or other devices. One of the major
crises of the Seventies, as I see it, will result as administrators attempt to move faculty from a role of
structural authority to one of sapiental authority. Under structural authority you have the right to tell
people something because of your position as teacher
or professor; under sapiental authority you have the
right because of your knowledge. Many faculty members are psychologically unable to make this transition.

C & UB: How did Robert Theobald become so open to
new ideas? Is this something unique with you or is
there a process that we can learn from and copy?

Theobald: I'm still not nearly as open as I'd wish, but it is true that change is always introduced at the periphery. If one has a different reality structure one sees things that appear to be crazy to other people living in the present reality structure. I was brought up in four countries: India, and my Indian friends assure me that my writing has a good lot of Indian thinking in it, England, France and the United States. It is because of this, I think, that it is almost impossible for me to look at anything in one way.

C & UB: A portion of "Teg's 1994, " a book that you and your wife wrote about the future of society and education, follows this interview. What were you and she trying to say in that book; what was your major motivating purpose in writing the book?

Theobald: With, or without, mankind's active participation, society is moving through the transition from the Industrial Era into the Communications Era. Teg, a woman of 20, in 1994, represents the kind of personality which could develop from this training and experience. Both authors were born in the Twenties, a time of technological transition, when an embryo Twentieth-Century technology, strong enough to be culturally destructive but too weak to provide organization, was supplemented and frequently replaced by psychological control.

Teg's personality is partly a product of 50 more years of the new technology. In her experience, technological organization has been established; she, therefore, meets her problems with a technic, not a smile. She would regard us as amiable, in-

competents, facing situations with misplaced gallantry,
when we should be applying technology to find a solution.
We find Teg cold and colorless on the surface, a main
protagonist who is less interesting than other personalities in the book. However, we believe the seeds of
the Teg-type personality are present now. If society
wishes for warm, sensitive, imaginative personalities
in 1994 or 1996 the effort must be made now.

Ever since he published "Men and Free Markets" in 1962
Robert Theobald's name has been associated with the
concept of the guaranteed income. Although he still
considers himself an economist, in the last several
years Mr. Theobald has lectured extensively and written books on psychological, societal and economic
systems for creating alternative societies.

School Around the Bend

Peter F. Drucker

THE SCHOOL OF TOMORROW WILL BE NEITHER
BEHAVIORISTIC NOR COGNITIVE, NEITHER
CHILD-CENTERED NOR DISCIPLINE-CENTERED.
IT WILL BE ALL OF THESE

We all know that the American school is in crisis.
People even talk of de-schooling America, and
foresee a future in which there will be no school
at all. This is not going to happen. But there certainly is ahead of us a long period of turbulence,
of re-thinking fundamentals and of building school
systems very different from any we have yet seen.

It is therefore important to realize that--beneath the
rhetoric and confusion--we really do understand the
problem. We know why the school is in crisis. We
know why what American education tomorrow should
look like. And we can guess where new, important
concepts will become practice.

The first thing to say--and it cannot be said too often--
is that the school is not in crisis just because it is
suddenly doing worse. Today's school does no poorer
a job than it did yesterday; the school has simply done
a terribly poor job all along. But what we tolerated in
the past we no longer can tolerate.

MISERY. That yesterday's school was a place that children loved and in which they learned is sheer delusion. There is scarcely one autobiography of the last 300 years in which school years are years of happiness. School was a place of misery, of boredom, of suffering, where, as every schoolmaster knew, only one of every 10 students learned anything at all. The rest were dunces. Nor did any college student around the turn of the century expect to learn much. One went to college because it led to a professional career, or because it was the socially acceptable thing to do, to make valuable connections. Learning was for a few grinds who were at best tolerated by their classmates. So, it is not that the school has become worse. Rather, the school has suddenly assumed such importance for the individual, for the community, for the economy and for society, that we cannot suffer the traditional, time-honored incompetence of the educational system. That students riot is nothing new. But that they riot because courses are not relevant is not only new, it's healthy.

WAY. Only yesterday school was, at best, a peripheral experience--for most, it was one or two or three summer terms of a few weeks each. (It had nothing to do with "education, " by the way; the highly educated people of that time were not, of necessity, those who had sat long in school. One acquired education--and mighty few did--by reading on one's own. This was true of Lincoln, as of most of the great persons of our history and of the history of Europe.) But today the child is expected to spend most of his childhood (even infancy), adolescence and early adulthood in school.

Part 1

In the past the family and the job were the educators.
Most youngsters   left school before they were 15;
much earlier they had begun to work on the family
farm or in the family shop. School was incidental;
lack of formal schooling was, at most, a slight handi-
cap. One could be a perfectly good farmer or a perfectly good carpenter--or even, as in the armies of
the Napoleonic wars, a perfectly good general--with-
out being able to write more than one's name.

ACCESS. I happen to come from a family with a
tradition of college, a family of lawyers and doctors.
Yet when   I told my father at the end of my high
school days, 40 years ago, that I did not plan to go
on to college but wanted to take a job instead, I was
not considered a dropout. I became an apprentice-
clerk in an export firm. And among my fellow apprentice-clerks were the sons of a distinguished historian
the son of a supreme-court judge, and the son of one
of the world's leading bankers--none of them considered   a dropout.

Today, access to careers, to most opportunities,
and to education is through the school. We expect
of the school--and it is a new expectation that no
school has met before--that most if not all students
will really learn   something. It is because this is
such a novel demand--and so historically irrational--
that the school is in crisis today.

We expect a person to find in school his basic experiences   and the knowledge foundation for his life. Above
all, we expect school to be the formal--exclusive--
channel to career and opportunity. I take a dim view

of our worship of the diploma. It is a despicable idol;
even money or success is worthier. But we depend
on the diploma, so we rightly demand that the schools
perform better.

BURDEN. At the same time, the school increasingly
becomes central to community, economy and society.
Rightly or wrongly, we demand that the school solve
America's oldest deepest, and most intractable problem of conscience, the problem of race relations. We
do not really expect of any other institution that it be
truly integrated. The school was not designed for this
load, and the teacher is not equipped to bear it. Both
probably do better at it than they get credit for doing.

We spend today more than 10 cents of every dollar of
gross national product on classroom education. It has
become our largest single expenditure. Schools and
colleges account for two thirds of the money, but non-
schools, government, businesses and professions
spend the other three or four cents on formal education. Education is thus the cost center of the American
economy. There is new concern with production and
achievement of the school, which always have been
pitifully low and which have shown no sign of increase.
As long as education was a marginal expense of society this did not matter, but now we care about productivity. Suddenly we ask questions of education.
Taxpayers resist educational spending for which they
see no results.

POWER. The organized knowledge that we expect organized schooling to impart has become part of the
foundation of our society.

In 1900 we ceased to be an agrarian and rural society and became an urban and industrial one. We are now becoming a knowledge society. We have centered in the educational complex all of the basic problems of our society, all of the basic issues--all of the concerns with ends and means, with beliefs and values, with relations between people and groups, with power, authority and legitimacy.

The educator now has power--perhaps this is the most unprecedented change of all. The schoolmaster decides when Johnny goes into third grade, whether Johnny should have access to opportunity, achievement and success. And the schoolmaster's decision to put Johnny in a slow track cannot be appealed; only rarely is it reconsidered. The educator has power that this society has never before been willing to grant to anybody. So far it is power without responsibility. The educator does not even know its extent; he has yet to think through what his responsibility is, to whom he should hold himself accountable.

The schools see themselves as they once were: a fleeting, not very important experience for the great majority, a vocational preparation for the learned professions for a small minority. The curriculum focuses on a small, narrow sector--the purely verbal. Educators look today for the very same things monks looked for 800 years ago when they trained scribes for the monastery or for the King's service.

The greater part of a person is not nourished in school. In the past those who showed no taste for the curriculum could go into arts and crafts, farm, factory or workshop. When I began work, I was one of the first apprentice-clerks who had finished secondary school. At that it was quite a scandal that an old firm like mine hired secondary-school graduates when everybody else had always gone to work at age 14. Traditionally, only the dumb members of the old merchant and banker families—in Boston as well as in Europe--stayed in school to become either lawyers or preachers.

So, the crisis of the schools is a problem of growth, less than one of failure. It is, nonetheless, real. It requires new, fundamental thinking and new, fundamental structure--from curriculum to teaching methods, from goals and objectives to responsibility, accountability and performance. Thank God, we are in for a turbulent time. At the same time new knowledge has undermined the school's intellectual foundations.

GIVENS. School in every country has been based on assumptions:
1) learning is a separate and distinct "intellectual" activity.
2) learning goes on in a separate organ, the mind, divorced from the body or the emotions.
3) learning is divorced from doing--indeed opposed to it; at best, it is preparation for doing; and
4) learning, because it is preparation, is for the young.

The time for learning was the stage at which the human being was deemed sufficiently mature to have "rational understanding" but not mature enough to do productive work. And one stopped learning as soon as one began doing. Today we know that learning is a continuous biological process. It begins at conception and ends only at death. Learning is not reserved for those who are

too old to play and too young to work. There is no
difference at all between the way the infant learns
and the way the adult learns. There is only one learning process.

We further assume that learning is not the exclusive
province of the mind or the intellect. It engages the
whole person, the hand, the eye, the muscle, the
brain.

And so the idea that at school one learns, while
everyplace else one does, is becoming untenable.

No one can tell what will happen in the schools this
year or next. But we already know reasonably well
where we should come out:

Tomorrow's school will have no rejects: it must guarantee every child a high minimum of accomplishment
in fundamental skills.

We no longer can talk of "dumb" or "lazy" children.
Almost every child learns, by age three or four,
basic skills that are infinitely more complex and more
difficult than anything we try to teach in school. Even
the least-endowed normal child learns the language,
for example. We will expect tomorrow's schools to
help each child acquire other, lesser skills, just as
we expect every family to enable a child to learn to
speak and to walk.

The schools must utilize the individual's own rhythm,
his own learning speed, his own pattern. This too, we
have learned by watching the infant acquire his basic
skills. No two children learn to speak the same way.
One child experiments for hours with sounds and ap-

parently does not tire. The next child plays with
sounds for 10 minutes, then shifts to something else,
then 10 minutes later comes back to playing with
sounds again, and so on.

The traditional lock step of education once was a necessity when the teacher had 30 or 50 children. He
had to impose the same pattern on all of them--or
thought he did. Certainly with today's tools, this no
longer is so--even in large classes.

The traditional school is labor--intensive; it has
neither tools nor capital equipment. We have invested
little more than $100 per student--except in medical
schools, physics laboratories and such--as against
the $30,000 or $40,000 or $50,000 the modern com-
munications company invests per employee. We have
relied on labor, which meant that the teacher's con-
venience had to be imposed on the entire class. Yet
teachers were both underpaid and underused. American education tomorrow will require a great deal more
by way of tools than we have had.

Today's school is still the school of the scribes. We
are beset by verbal arrogance, contemptuous of whatever is not reading, writing, or arithmetic. And yet
one look should show us a world in which verbal skills
are not the only productive ones. They are necessary
a foundation. But the purely verbal skills are not
necessarily the central performance skill when electronic media carry the main information load.

People are endowed differently in different areas, but
today's school dismisses three quarters of human en-
dowments as irrelevant. This is inhuman and stupid.

It is also incompatible with the realities of our
economy and our society. We need craftsmen in
thousands of areas; everywhere we need people
with excellence in one area--and not necessarily
a verbal one. We will expect the school to find the
individual's real strength, challenge it, and make
it productive.

The school of tomorrow will be neither behavioristic nor cognitive, neither child-centered nor
discipline-centered. It will be all of these.

These old controversies have been phonies all
along. We need the behaviorist's triad of practice/
reinforcement/feedback to lodge learning in memory.
We need purpose, decision, values, understanding--
the cognitive categories, lest learning be mere behavior, activity rather than action.

The English open classroom, now widely copied in
this country, usually is considered cognitive and
child-centered. It is. But it also is one of the first
rigorous applications of behaviorism to large numbers of human learners. The child does indeed learn
his or her way there. He programs himself according
to his own pattern, rhythm, speed and sequence. But
he programs himself also according to a strict behaviorist scheme. What he is working (or playing) on
is determined by the tools, playthings and experiences
offered. Reinforcements and rewards are built in at
every step. Above all, the school predetermines the
norms of achievement as rigorously as a scientist
lays them down for a rat in a maze. And the child
does not move on to the next level until he attains
and retains the norm.

Whatever one thinks of the contracts on the organization

of specific skills, they are also both behaviorist and cognitive. Together, teacher and child work out a plan and follow it with a verbal or written contract that commits the child to work toward his own goal. In their methodology, these contracts focus strictly on behavior and discipline. But the main argument for performance contracts is strictly cognitive: what the child needs is self-confidence--the capacity to feel that he is the master of his environment--that is, the human development that comes with achievement and social approbation. The greatest of the cognitivists--Johann Heinrich Pestalozzi or Jean Piaget--could not have put better the case for the child-centered approach.

The traditional issues of educational methodology and philosophy are simply different tools in the same toolbox. Indeed, they may be only the obverse and reverse of the same coin.

While it is moving out of the Middle Ages academically, tomorrow's school also must integrate itself into the community and become an integrator of the community. As the school system exploded in this century it had to become professional. But in the process it ceased to be part of its community.

A great deal can be said against the rigidity of the small college of the mid-19th century with its narrow religious blinkers and its authoritarian structure. But it was part of a denominational community. Today's larger university may be intellectually richer, freer, more rewarding, but it is no community and it has no community. The students of 1870 complained bitterly but they didn't feel alienated.

The same was true of the small school in the rural community; in fact, the teacher often felt smothered and dominated by the community.

I do not advocate a return to what we had a century ago. But we must bring the community back into the school. American education will have to think through who its constituents are and get across to them--students, teachers, taxpayers, parents, alumni and prospective employers--what they can expect from the school, and also what the school can expect of them.

One way or another education will become accountable for performance. I do not know how one measures performance in education. First you have to know what the objectives and goals are. If the first job of an elementary school is to have the children learn to read, one can measure performance easily. But if the school at the same time is also to socialize, to make civilized human beings out of children, to develop the whole person--prepare him for work and life--then no one can measure performance. The school will be expected to think through its goals, get them accepted, and be accountable for them. If it fails to do so, measurement standards will be imposed from the outside, and the educators who protest have only themselves to blame. Schools are too powerful and too important; they must be responsible for performance.

Finally, and most important, American education must acknowledge that learning is lifelong--it does not stop when one starts working. The most important learning, the most important true education, is the continuing education of educated, achieving adults.

The educator has not yet accepted the idea of continuing education. Most schoolmasters believe that one can learn only when one is young and only before five in the afternoon. Most of them still believe that learning is for the immature, that is is not serious enough for adults. The realization that adults continue to learn will have a pro- found impact on the structure curriculum, methods and position of traditional education. We will demand much more from it, but we will no longer consider it the edu- cation.

These changes in tomorrow's education may come to pass first, in the continuing education of adults. The restraints are lowest there--no school boards and no teacher associations, no taxpayers, no schools of edu- cation, no concerned parents, no headlines. Students control continuing education--it depends on their moti- vation and achievement. It is decentralized, thus exper- imentation is easy. It has far fewer problems with bud- gets, especially when business, Government agencies, or other large employers support or run it. It can spend capital. And, continuing education already practices, though on a narrow, mostly vocational front, most of the basic principles of tomorrow's school. It is a working model, on a small scale, but it is proof of what we can achieve. It is also the most rapidly growing segment of organized education.

Schools are very old. But the identification of learning with school is very recent--hardly more than a century old. That so far we have not delivered on the promise that the school will be the learning institution is hardly surprising. It is, perhaps, far more surprising that we already know, if only in rough outline, what the school needs to be to live up to its importance, its power, and its responsibility.

Peter F. Drucker is Professor of Management at New York University's Graduate School of Business.

Part II

FORECASTING AND SPECIFYING EDUCATIONAL FUTURES

*We must cease to be mere spectators
in our own ongoing history
and participate with determination
in moulding the future.*

OLAF HELMER

**"Prospects for an Institute
for the future"**

Anticipating the Future
and Evaluating Alternatives

Commission on Educational Planning

.... STUDIES OF THE FUTURE OUGHT TO BE AN
INTEGRAL PART OF SCHOOLING.

Planning always involves some view of the future.
Thus, the interrelationship between educational planning and other futures-forecasting is reciprocal:each
affects the other. Usually it is assumed that the future will be much like the present, or that present
trends will continue unabated into the future. For
short-range planning these assumptions have sufficient validity to render them useful for decision
making. This is particularly true for specific quantifiable variables. The children who will be in school
five years from now have already been born; the skilled
technicians required 10 years from now are already
in school. Projections of enrollments, and of space
and dollar requirements can often be made on the
basis of available trend data.

The generation of predictions and projections for
short-range planning has been greatly enhanced by
computer simulations. Through the use of quantitative models, it is possible to simulate items like
enrollments, costs and personnel requirements under
different assumptions. The range of models available
is now substantial. Some depict flows of students
through an entire educational system, while others
are geared to institutional resource needs. The Organ-

Reprinted from A Choice of Futures, a report of the
Commission on Educational Planning for the Cabinet
Committee on Education, Edmonton, Alberta, Canada.

ization for Economic Cooperation and Development
(OECD) in Paris has developed a flexible simulation
option model that forecasts educational outputs and
demands during future periods of time. This model
can also be used for sensitivity analysis; that is, for
determining what the effect would be of variations in
selected factors. Models such as these should be a-
dapted or developed for simulating various quantitative aspects of the Alberta system for schooling,
provincially and locally. To a considerable extent
this would involve only an extension and refinement
of work that has already been initiated at Lethbridge
Community College and by some university and government departments.

Techniques are also emerging for the systematic exploration of social futures in long-term perspective.
The best known is the Delphi technique. Essentially
a refinement of brainstorming, the Delphi technique
progressively sharpens forecasts by seeking agreement within a group of experts on a step-by-step
basis. It can contribute much to the formulation of
educational and social goals where intuitive thinking
is valuable and where consensus is important. Scenario writing can be used to outline the steps through
which some selected condition can be reached, and
identifying some of the critical choice points in the
evolutionary process. Cross impact analysis is a promising technique for considering the interactions among
predicted events. The attention given these approaches
should be equal to that given the seemingly more tan-
gible quantitative simulation techniques. Even though
some may think we presently lack the knowledge necessary to bring about a preferred future, the development

of futures-forecasts can at least sensitize us to avoiding
the undesired, to striving toward the preferred, and to
extending our time horizons as the present moves more
rapidly into the future.

Elsewhere in this report it is argued that studies of the
future ought to be an integrated part of schooling. To
provide a knowledge base for such studies is another
reason for seeing that an anticipatory look-out capacity
is built into the planning process. And if a two-way flow
of information between planner-futurologists and citi-
zen-learners were cultivated, then the ideal of partici-
patory planning would move one giant step closer to
reality.

Every decision-maker dreams of the day when he will
be able to lay out all alternatives before action, to carry
out a complete analysis of the consequences of choosing
the various alternatives, and then to select the best alternative before taking any action. Like most dreams,
this one dissolves when exposed to the light of day. The
extent to which the decision process can be so rationalized
is still limited. A high degree of uncertainty may be
attached to various outcomes, and the selection of an
alternative may be only a best guess based upon highly
subjective judgments. Such a departure from the ideal
state does not deny the possibility of planning or negate
planning since the process also involves reviewing, evaluating and correcting courses of action. Even though the
decision-maker may not be able to evaluate his alternatives completely in advance, he can still take action and
evaluate the alternative which he has selected after it has
been implemented.

Substantial progress has been made in recent years in
conceptual and technical approaches to the evaluation of

educational programs. Of particular interest are those that are well-suited to management decisions. These approaches emphasize the evaluation of all stages of the decision process: assessment and evaluation of the situation of inputs, of the process of implementation, and of final outcomes. The evaluation process requires that standards and criteria for determining worth be established at all stages of the activity. These broadened conceptions of evaluation should become an integral part of the analysis required in educational planning and of the life-style in our institutions for schooling.

The efficiency objective in educational planning results in giving high priority to economic criteria in making decisions. Consequently, techniques such as cost/benefit analysis, cost-effectiveness analysis, and cost- quality studies have achieved high levels of visibility. Although these techniques can be a useful aid to decision-making, there is also a possibility that their contribution to educational planning has been over-rated. Any over-statement of the contribution of such analyses to educational planning can be attributed both to overanxious planners in search of techniques, and an overly narrow conception of the functions of schooling on the part of those who carry out such analysis. In any event, some elaboration of cost/benefit analysis, cost-effectiveness and cost-quality studies may be helpful in placing these techniques in perspective. The distinctions that are made among the three may not be universally accepted and are not presented as being definitive. However, they do serve to identify essential differences.

The general concept of cost/benefit analysis is highly rational and most appealing to the decision-maker who must choose among alternatives: array costs of a course of action on one side, its benefits on the other, and then

decide on the basis of the cost/benefit ratio. Often this
is done intuitively by many people when facing choices
in their daily lives. The attempt to raise the analysis
to a more explicit and quantified level does increase its
rigor, but it also greatly restricts the scope of the variables that enter into the analysis. In order to establish a cost/benefit ratio only quantifiable variables can
be considered, and these are usually expressed in terms
of expected lifetime earnings of individuals who have acquired particular forms of training. The cost/benefit of
the training is then expressed as a rate of return on the
investment in the training program. A slight variation
is to determine the present value of the investment rather than the rate-of-return. It can be seen, therefore,
that all cost/benefit studies share one central assumption. They all postulate a link between schooling and
earnings in later life. But schooling helps people develop a variety of skills. They use these skills in their
working environment as well as in many other activities. Up until now, cost/benefit analysis has been confined almost exclusively to the benefits accruing in people's working lives. If such studies are to reflect the true
rate of return to schooling, it is obvious that ways must
be found to measure benefits in other facets of life.

A broader range of benefits is usually considered in cost-
effectiveness analysis which is applied when several
methods are available for achieving the same objective.
Relative costs and relative effectiveness using numerical
indices of different methods--such as instruction by
television and instruction by more conventional methods-
can be determined and the resultant information used in
decision-making. Obviously, if one of the methods has
lower costs and higher effectiveness in terms of the

The Delphi Forecasting Method

W. Timothy Weaver

DELPHI...OPERATES ON THE PRINCIPLE THAT
SEVERAL HEADS ARE BETTER THAN ONE IN
MAKING SUBJECTIVE CONJECTURES ABOUT THE
FUTURE, AND THAT EXPERTS.....WILL MAKE
CONJECTURES BASED UPON RATIONAL JUDGMENT
AND SHARED INFORMATION RATHER THAN MERELY
GUESSING, AND WILL SEPARATE HOPE FROM
LIKELIHOOD IN THE PROCESS

It has simply been the case in education that the time
lag between initial policy decision and measurable
impact is very long; that is, investments in education
are not recognized in the short run. Futhermore,
during the time interval between policy decision and
observable impact, social conditions influencing
schools will change. Here-and-now educational choices
have both long-term consequences and immediate
impacts. Yet short-term rather than long-term policy matters dominate educational thinking.

Two conclusions follow. First, educational thinking must
take into account more of the future than is typical now.
Alternative plans, policies, and research programs must
be assessed in relation to the most systematic conjectures that can be developed about the future environment
in which schools can be expected to exist. Secondly,
factors that are viewed as decisive in the current state of
affairs may well not be the most significant factors to con-

sider for the long-term commitment of educational
resources, or in shaping educational plans and policies. The present eruption and impact of widespread
student dissent was not generally anticipated in policy planning a decade ago. It follows that educational
planning and policy decisions must incorporate the use
of forecasting tools whose purpose it would be to continually conduct and assess studies of the future.

The question I want to examine in the remainder of
this article is, On what grounds can educators select
among forecasting tools? Several quasi-scientific
tools are on the market today comprising, in effect,
a policy planners' forecasting kit. At a minimum, the
value of such methodologies cannot be weighed apart
from some reasonable understanding of the processes
by which they aid in producing forecasts. I shall return to this point later. As well, in order to effectively evaluate forecasting methods, one must be able
to test the plausibility of the forecast which results.
Plausibility demands that the forecast include some
explanatory quality. A forecast is simply a proposition that one can evaluate. Instead, it is the reasonableness of those arguments and explanations which
support the propositions. The propositions must be
accompanied by the author's logical warrants, reasons, assumptions, and grounds. I shall return later
to this point as well.

WHAT DELPHI IS

The Delphi Technique is an intuitive methodology for
organizing and sharing "expert" forecasts about the
future. Its original use was to establish a chronology
of scientific and technological events and to judge when

the events might occur through the speculations of several experts. Delphi has been justified primarily on the grounds that it prevents professional status and high position from forcing judgments in certain directions as frequently occurs when panels of experts meet. The intention was to assure that changes in estimates reflected rational judgment, not the influence of certain opinion leaders.

Typically, the procedure includes a questionnaire, mailed to respondents who remain anonymous to one another. Respondents first generate several rather concise statements of events, and in the second round give estimates as to the probability of each event occuring at a given date in the future. Once the respondents have given their answers, the responses are collated and returned to each respondent who then is invited to revise his estimates. The third-round responses are made with the knowledge of how others felt regarding the occurrence of each event. Again, the responses are assembled and reported back to the participants. If a respondent's estimate does not fall within the interquartile range of all conjectures, he is asked to justify his position, whether or not he wishes to change his position.

More recently, the technique has been extended to include questions about how familiar the participants are with the events. Respondents are also occasionally asked to rate the desirability of the events, should they occur. In addition, respondents are asked to give some statements about what impacts the events might have. Still another question now being asked is what possible "interventions" might be developed to either enhance or reduce the probability that an event would occur.

Delphi has been tried in educational planning on the assumption that one way to improve the formulation of educational policies and plans is to expand the awareness among educators of alternative future options as well as the expectations they hold about such options. However, that requires some considerable understanding of the processes of future thinking, as well as policy thinking, and the development of tools that facilitate a more complex consideration of the future than now exists. The thrust so far has been to force attention to assumptions, values, goals, and factors which might lead to one or another social objective.

One of the earliest uses of Delphi in educational thinking was Helmer's study incorporated as part of the 1965 Kettering project to elicit preference judgments from a panel of education experts and experts in various fields related to education. The purpose was to compile a list of preferred goals for possible federal funding. Just what value this study had is left in doubt by the experiments. Helmer concludes, "Although we believe that the compilation of a large number of ideas for possible educational innovations has served a useful purpose, not too much weight should be given to substantive findings resulting from these pilot studies. "

Two additional Delphis have been conducted and reported as experiments to elicit preference statements from educators or those with a direct interest in education. The studies were considerably more foced than Helmer's experiment. Cyphert and Gant used Delphi as an opinion

questionnaire to elicit preferences from the faculty of
the School of Education at the University of Virginia
and other concerned parties. Anderson used Delphi
in a similar way in Ohio but limited the focus to a
county school district.

In the Anderson study, statements were obtained from
teachers, board members, administrators, and selected educational experts. The statements clustered in
two sets: client services and organizational adaptation.
Using three Delphi questionnaires, priorities were
assigned to each compiled set of goal statements independently, using "zero sum" logic.

In both the Virginia study and the Ohio study, most of
the change in priorities occurred after the first modal
distribution was reported back to all respondents. Subsequent rounds failed to produce significant changes.
The greatest disagreement on particular items in the
Virginia study was on preparation of teachers at the
graduate level without prior experience and on promot-
ing statewide ùniformity of curriculum. The former
item, preparation of teachers without experience, was
ranked among the top 10 by the groups as a whole, but
lowest by organization leaders and politicians. The
latter item, a ,uniform curriculum was ranked high by
the nonteacher organization and low by the university
and expert groups.

These education studies differ in principle from the
original use of Delphi. In the three studies, respondents were asked to focus on what they would like to
see happen, rather than what is likely to happen. However, it is unclear how that difference in focus would
change the outcome of either type of experiment. It

is not possible at the moment to precisely identify
Delphi statements which reflect rational judgment
as opposed to feelings of desirability. When the task
is speculating on the future, just what assumptions
underlie one's responses is unclear--that is, unless
those assumptions are specifically and systematically flushed out.

In other studies, Delphi was used in essentially its
"pure" form to make forecasts about the future of
education. As a pilot experiment at the San Diego
meeting of the National Conference of Professors
of Educational Administration, a Delphi was conducted by staff from the Institute for the Future, Middletown, Connecticut; and the Educational Policy Research
Center, Syracuse University Research Corporation.
The major purpose was to collect conjectures about
prospective developments which might have an impact
on educational administration, their probably dates
of occurrence, the desirability of such developments
should they occur, and their potential interventions.

Delphi was also used to develop long-range forecasts
stemming from social indicators in a study conducted
by the Institute for the Future and sponsored primarily
by the Syracuse Educational Policy Research Center.
The areas of concern were urbanization, international
relations, conflict in society and law enforcement,
national political structure, values, and the impact of
technology on government and society. The project was
part of a larger continuing methodological and substantive study of the future environment in which educational policies enacted in the near future might be expected
to have some impact. The study was conceived not to
prepare a detailed description of the future, but instead

to examine expectations about the future held by persons well informed in several domains of the social sciences. The study was intended to be only an initial step and not a final piece of research.

A number of difficulties were encountered in the research. First, there was no comprehensive theororetical framework to guide the inquiry. Second, and fundamentally, the social science expectations did not carry the crispness of language and precision of judgment that the more rationalized process of technological change seemed to have in the original uses of Delphi. For instance, just when electric power plants driven by thermonuclear fuel will become widespread is a development controlled by several "knowable" technological factors. The same cannot be said of when alienation and impersonality of urban living will reach its maximum. Indeed we do not even know what it means to speak of a "maximum" in this case. Third, the data base available to social science forecasting is shifting and often more unreliable than technological data. For example, data on the percentage of urban minorities is often not precise and its collection a matter of serious controversy. Fourth, even with the best of statistics, judgments in the social domain are subject to considerable variance due to disagreement on the meaning of indicators; thus forecasts are more likely biased by personal values than may be true of technological forecasts.

Finally, Delphi has been modified and linked together with other tools, not for the purpose of producing intuitive forecasts, but for the purpose of modifying the awareness, assumptions, and skills of the persons making the forecasts. For example, Sandow construc-

ted a simulation exercise which links together in a
logical flow of activities the basic principles of Delphi
cross-impact matrix, scenario writing, and analysis
of future histories.

There have been a number of other "first-step" efforts elsewhere to recast forecasting tools. These
efforts are largely unreported to date. The Ghetto
1984 game developed by Jose Villegas at Cornell
University   bears noting as well as the Delphi Exploration game developed at the University of Illinois.

In the University of Illinois project, initiated by
Charles E. Osgood, Delphi was used to create a com-
puterized gaming device called Delphi Exploration.
The general pattern of the game followed that of Future,
a parlor-type game developed by Olaf Helmer and
Theodore Gordon. Statements from prior Delphi research were used in the computer game. In addition,
the cross-impact matrix has been added.   In Delphi
Exploration the players make investments in one set
of future events in an attempt to move ,undesirable
developments toward 0% probability while moving desirable developments toward 100% probablity. In the
Delphi II program now under development, the player
will be able to work   through time from the present
to some point in the future. In Delphi I, the operating
program, the player   simply tries to build what he
considers to be a desirable world in the year 2000.
It is the process through which players must go in
Delphi Exploration that its developers view as the primary teaching objective.

TOWARD AN EFFECTIVE CRITIQUE

Let me return to the points made earlier. In order
to effectively critique the Delphi method, one must
consider both its process and its product. Here my
focus on process is upon the way people are asked
to handle information about the future, while my
concern with product is a concern with plausibility.

Within this context, let me further identify the
"family" of forecasting tools I am concerned with in
this article. Although I have focused on Delphi specifically, it should be understood that Delphi is only
one of several "intuitive" exploratory methods. Other
methods include future history analysis, scenario
writing, and cross-impact matrices.

These tools share some common properties. They
employ collective opinion or subjective judgment
as basic inputs to the forecasting process in lieu of
quantifiable data. In effect, they operate on the principle that several heads are better than one in making
subjective conjectures about the future, and that experts, within a controlled intuitive process, will make
conjectures based upon rational judgment and shared
information rather than merely guessing, and will
separate hope from likelihood in the process. That
is, it is assumed that experts are experts because they
are objective, take into account new or discrepant
information, and construct logically sound deduc-
tions about the future based upon a thorough and dis-
ciplined understanding of particular phenomena and
how they relate. Simply put, the methods are non-
data based and rely on collective expert judgment.

Futhermore, the forecasts do not begin, as do extrapolations, with a demonstration of how future events grow out of specific present or past conditions. That is, these forecasts are not so much projections as they are quantum leaps into some future time frame in which one is left to find his way backward to the present. The plausibility of such forecasts cannot, therefore, be argued out on the basis of certain mathematically describably functions such as a Poisson curve or Baumol's Law. The resultant future proposition is testable only on the basis of some mode of reasonable explanation, that is, some theory, model, hypothesis, or logical or a priori argument or deduction.

It is therefore crucial that these tools heavily emphasize the explanations upon which the plausibility of the forecast rests. An intuitive forecast which carries with it no explanatory quality may be correct, but it would be trivial. That is the singular weakness of Delphi. Delphi forecasts have little substantive explanatory quality in their present form. The plausibility of the Delphi forecast as now construed can be argued only on the basis of expert consensus or agreement. But consensus alone is not a sufficient condition for arguing that a forecast is plausible and convincing. (It is not even a necessary condition.)

To strengthen this argument, it is self-evident that whatever we think about the future must be thought out in the absence of detailed knowledge about what the future will be. We can know neither the future in precise terms nor precisely what is best now for the future. These are matters of judgment, not fact. Such

a notion does not presume, however, that the future
cannot be a dimension of our thoughts, nor that those
thoughts cannot be translated into actions which have
some probablity of controlling or limiting the future.
In short, although a future event cannot be preor-
dained and has not yet occurred, because it has been
imagined its likelihood of occurring may well be
changed.

A statement about the future, or what one imagines
it to be, is in this sense like a work of art. It can only
be more or less accepted by the critic, but it cannot
be proved false. Therefore such statements can be
assessed as reasonable, but not necessarily on the
basis of their actual outcome. That is, a proposition
about the future may be said to be reasonable even if
what was foreseen turned out not to happen. It seemed
reasonable or plausible or convincing at the time it was
made. And even to the extent that propositions about the
future can be based upon empirical assumptions, they
still are matters of rational persuasion, not of evidence
which gives a scientific proof.

The educated policy implication underlying future studies is, therefore, that the meaning of any statement
about the future will be manifested only in what the statement convinces us the future can be made to be through
reasonable actions, not in what it will be. Therein lies
a fundamental source of conflict. What the future can
be or should be made to be differs drastically in the
minds of people. We all carry around a different set of
assumptions about the future. The failure to clarify
and share such assumptions is a failure of Delphi forecasts. Studying the future is in effect studying assumptions we hold about the future. Stripping bare the under-

lying assumptions about the future often reveals that (a) we present no alternatives. (b) our thoughts are based upon very naive and weak arguments, and (c) our judgments are the product of linear thinking. As a result, forecasts fail to convince. They offer no reasonable options. It seems fundamental that fore-casts will have little value to policy makers unless they open options.

The nature of the Delphi method then ought to be such that certain rather important distinctions could be made about forecasts and their underlying assumptions. For instance, we often fail to distinguish what is desirable from what seems plausible about the future. When we talk about something being desirable in the future, we use such words as "hope" or "goal." When we speak of plausibility, we use such words as "expect, " "prob-ability, " or "likelihood. " There is a fundamental dis-tinction to be made, although often it is not. The pur-pose for making such a distinction is to separate fore-casts of what seems "likely"--given certain factors-- from what we would "like" to see happen, or like to keep from happening. It is not clear how one can dis-criminate between Delphi forecasts that are the pro-ducts of "hope" and those that are "probable. " It is clear, however, that hope or desirability interferes with and to a considerable extent influences judgments about future events.

A second fundamental distinction needs to be made in the absence of actually knowing in detail just what the future will be, one can either guess or judge. The very basis of the Delphi forecasting process is opinion as to when an event is likely to occur. It seems important in establishing the plausibility of such forecasts, that opinion be distinguishable as rational judgment rather than guesswork. Delphi, at present, can render no such distinction, because the arguments which support an opinion are not emphasized unless the opinion is contrary to the group norm.

Let me continue to focus for a moment on process. What we know about how the mind constructs images of the future remains rather puny, but the fundamental assumptions which are generally held about Delphi seem questionable. For instance, the Delphi Technique was created to prevent professional status and high position from forcing judgments in certain directions when panels of experts met. The intention was to assure that through questionnaires, changes in estimates would reflect rational judgment and therefore not be subject to social psychological factors. Empirical evidence tends to show the naivete of such an assumption. Three independently conducted studies suggest that within the Delphi procedure individuals who "swing" in from wide ranges to more narrow ranges do so less on the basis of rational argument, examination of evidence, or review of assumptions than because decision-making strategies of certain persons are subject to change as the task is perceived to be less ambiguous, and on account of certain personality factors such as fundamental needs and integrative complexity. These findings, of course, are not unexpected, and generally support the studies of several other investigators. It also seems clear that subjective judgments of even very complex or abstract thinkers may be considerably influenced by their feelings of desirability regarding the future events in question. The assumption that "experts," who may be presumed to be complex thinkers, bring to bear "cool analysis" in their judgments about the future is questionable in light of this finding.

Still focusing for the moment on process, just what do

we know about how people think about the future?
From the research reviewed in earlier papers   I
have drawn the following summary observations.

The psychological studies of future perspective and
personality traits strongly suggest that concepts and
perceptions held about oneself and society are interrelated and reflective of thoughts about the future.
Conceptual level, alienation, anxiety, social devi-
ancy, emotional instability, and schzophrenia--all
indicators of particular ways of perceiving and relating to society--impinge upon one's future cogni-
tion. Numerous studies showed that these indicators were sufficiently powerful to distinguish perceptions about the future--particularly when such
perceptions involve estimating how long something
would take or involve foreseeing some state or state
of affairs.

It follows that persons with different kinds of "self-
structures"   (needs, attitudes, beliefs, etc.)would
hold different perceptions about the present as well
as the future, and thus produce different kinds of
forecasts about the future. This statement appears
to be rather evident. How to shape it into a research-
able set of questions is not as evident because exogenous variables also impinge upon judgments. For instance, the phrasing or complexity of a question, or
the influence of a group norm, even though it may be
anonymous, may influence the judgments of certain
people. Whether or not the judgmental task is vague
or uncertain, or is perceived to be vague or uncertain, may also influence particular people to a considerable degree.

Research questions on forecasting methods must begin

to reflect some consideration of the interaction between dispositional factors and the conditions in the experiment. Among the more important questions are: How do differences in judgments about the future reflect differences in the self-structures of the people who make the judgments? And consequently, how will differences in estimates be shaped by exogenous variables such as complexity and ambiguity of the task? The failure to consider these questions is a persistent weakness of Delphi studies to date.

SUMMARY

Delphi, like the future it was intended to foretell, has not turned out to be what we expected. There are certain fundamental weaknesses of Delphi in its present form as a forecasting tool. Briefly, they have to do with interpreting the significance of "convergence" of opinion under the conditions imposed by Delphi. The observation that people tend to shift their estimates toward a group norm under conditions of iteration is a consistent and sound observation on the basis of several controlled experiments with Delphi. There is some very meager evidence which suggests that compression of estimates over rounds produces a final consensus closer to the "true" answer (when the consensus is taken as a median of the spread of estimates). This finding, however, is based upon evidence collected from very short-term predictions in the economic domain, and from experiments with almanac-type questions. Just how the findings can be generalized to Delphi's which cover a 30-year extension of the future is unknown. Moreover, to make such a generalization is irrelevant to an understanding of plausibility as discussed above. Yet interpreting the social-psychological significance of the convergency that does occur with such opinion is important in understanding how the mind processes information about the future. Once we can understand more clearly how the mind formulates images of the future, we will be in a better position to improve upon the process of constructing rational and plausible forecasts.

Any consideration of the future of education should attempt to clarify what we can reasonably expect to make happen or not expect to make happen. Rather than a focus on "accuracy," the focus might better be on "plausibility" or reasonableness of forecasts. In that sense Delphi at present comes up short because there is little emphasis on the grounds or arguments which might convince policy makers of the forecasts" reasonableness. There are insufficient procedures to distinguish hope from likelihood. Delphi at present can render no rigorous distinction between reasonable judgment and mere guessing; nor does it clearly distinguish priority and value statements from rational arguments, nor feelings of confidence and desirability from statements of probability.

Of equally great importance, however, our research also leads us to conclude that Delphi, in combination with other tools, is a very potent device for teaching people to think about the future of education in much more complex ways than they ordinarily would. When we understand this use of Delphi we may find that it is a useful instrument for something more important than what it was designed for, namely, a general teaching strategy. What this means is that initially the way to get educators to make better decisions--decisions which account for alternative consequences--is to enhance their capacity to think in complex ways about the future, and Delphi seems ideally suited to such a purpose. Indeed, educators may find in Delphi and other forecasting tools a better pedagogy.

To sum up quickly, although Delphi was originally intended as a forecasting tool, its more promising educational application seems to be in the following areas: (a) a method for studying the process of thinking about the future, (b) a pedagogical tool or teaching tool which forces people to think about the future in a more complex way than they ordinarily would, and (c) a planning tool which may aid in probing priorities held by members and constituencies of an organization.

The future of education is uncertain. Its very historical justification is being questioned. When men perceive that uncertainty lies ahead, their concern with the future increases proportionately. Therefore, it is inevitable that more of the future be taken into account, but it is only through thoughtful study of forecasts and forecast tools that it can be taken into account reasonably.

W. Timothy Weaver is a research fellow at Syracuse University's Educational Policy Research Center. He wishes to thank Robert Bundy, guest lecturer at the University of Maryland and Syracuse University, and Thomas F. Green, co-director of the Educational Policy Research Center, for important contributions to this article.

Planning Amid Forces
for Institutional Change

Willis W. Harman

.... A FUNDAMENTAL TRANSFORMATION OF
(THE) MIND (METANOIA) appears necessary for
a desirable future. ....

In the work of this Center we have attempted to
construct a comprehensive set of "alternative
future histories" for this nation from now until
the year 2000.[1] (This was accomplished by devising an adequately rich coded description of the
state of society and then systematically examining
which sequence of these states are feasible for the
next 30 years.) The results of this analysis indicate
that the vast majority of the "future histories" so
constructed are clearly to be avoided if possible.
The reasons vary--from authoritarian government
to economic collapse, from ecological catastrophe
to exhaustion from continuous warfare.

It will be our purpose here to explore concisely (a)
the reasons for considering such a far-reaching cultural and institutional metamorphosis to be plausible
and perhaps even likely (though uncomfortable), (b)
the nature of the change, and (c) some of the most
important implications for our social institutions.

This paper was presented at the 1971 symposium
Planning in the Seventies, co-sponsored by the
Washington Chapter of the American Society for
Public Administration and the National Bureau of
Standards.

Let us first be explicit as regards the magnitude and
pervasiveness of the transformation being posited. This
is thoroughgoing systemic change, to a degree comparable at least with such historic transitions as the Fall
of Rome, the Reformation, and the Industrial Revolution, involving changes in basic cultural premises, the
root image of man-in-society, fundamental value postulates, and all aspects of social roles and institutions.

Lewis Mumford notes that there have probably been not
more than a half dozen profound transformations of Western society since primitive man. Each of these "has
rested on a new metaphysical and ideological base; or
rather, upon deeper stirrings and intuitions whose rationalized expression takes the forms of a new picture
of the cosmos and the nature of man."[2] I want clearly
to distinguish what we are hypothesizing from other
changes which are revolutionary in a social or political
sense but do not involve transformation of the basic,
implicit, unchallenged, taken-as-given metaphysic.
We might apply to it, by analogy, the Greek word for religious conversion, metanoia: "a fundamental transformation of mind."[3]

Bear in mind, I am not saying that metanoia must inex-
orably take place--rather, that is appears necessary for
a desirable future, that some cultural movement toward
its accomplishment is evident, and that our social and
political choices over the next few years may be fateful,
in that by fostering or repressing the forces for metanoia
they can drastically affect the future of the human experiment.

1. Necessity of paradigm change

It will be helpful to introduce another term. In his semi-

nal study of the structure of scientific revolutions T.
S. Kuhn[4] uses the term "dominant paradigm" to refer
to the basic way of perceiving, thinking, and doing,
associated with a particular vision of reality, largely
embodied in unquestioned, tacit understanding trans-
mitted primarily through examplars.

In historical retrospect we can see that a paradigm
which began its climb to dominance several centuries
ago, has since influenced all aspects of Western society. This industrial-state paradigm, sharply differing from the dominant paradigm of the Middle Ages,
is characterized by:

> Development and application of scientific method
> Wedding of scientific and technological advance
> Industrialization through division of labor
> Progress defined as technological and economic
> growth
> Man seeking control over nature; positivistic
> theory of knowledge
> Acquisitive materialism, work ethic, economic-
> man image

Born out of this paradigm are the fabulous products of
modern industrial organization and modern technology.
The beginnings of breakdown of the paradigm are dramatically shown in the fact that its successes underlie
all the serious social problems of our day. Table I
illustrates this. The left hand column lists the achieve-
ments of industrial society; the right hand column lists
the corresponding problems to which these have led.
These problems are ultimately unsolvable in the present
paradigm precisely because their origins are in the
success of that paradigm.

TABLE I

"Successes" of the technological era	Resulting problems of being "too successful"
Prolonging life span	Overpopulation; problems of aged
Arms-national defense	Hazard of mass destruction
Machine replacement of manual labor	Exacerbated unemployment
Advances in communication & transportation	Urbanization; "shrinking world"; vulnerability of society
Efficiency	Dehumanization of world of work
Power growth of systematized knowledge	Threats to privacy & freedoms; "knowledge barrier" to underclass
Affluence	Increased per capita environmental impact, pollution, energy shortage
Satisfaction of basic needs; ascendance up "need-level hierarchy"	World revolutions of "rising expectations", rebellion against "non-meaningful work, unrest among affluent students
Expanded power of human choice	Management breakdown as regards control of consequences of technological applications
Expanded wealth of developed nations	Intrinsically increasing gap between have and have-not nations
Development of pre-potent high-technology capability	Apparent economic necessity of war to use up output of "megamachine. "5

This breakdown of the industrial-state paradigm is at least fivefold:

1. It fails to promote further accomplishment of one of the most fundamental functions of a society, namely to provide each individual with an opportunity to contribute to the society and to be affirmed by it in return.

2. It fails to foster more equitable distribution of power, wealth, and justice.

3. It fails to foster socially responsible management of the development and application of technology.

4. It fails to provide goals which will enlist the deepest loyalties and commitments of the nation's citizens.

5. It fails to develop and maintain the habitability of the planet.

These failures are intrinsic, built into the paradigm itself and awaiting only the unfolding of consequences until they become critical. Population pressure, itself a consequence of the technology-aided prolonging a life span, alters the timetable, making problems crucial earlier than they might be if population were reduced. But population limiting alone will not resolve the problems. (This fact is immediately apparent if one imagines population to remain constant but affluence and consumption levels throughout the world to be raised to those presently enjoyed by the American upper middle class.)

II. An emerging "New Age" paradigm

Victor Ferkiss,[6] analyzing the unavoidable problems
to which the technological ethic leads, concludes that
the required "new guiding philosophy" must contain
three basic and essential elements. First it what he
terms a "new naturalism, " which affirms that man is
absolutely a part of a nature, a universe, that is always in the process of becoming. The second element,
a "new holism, " recognizes that "no part can be defined or understood save in relation to the whole. "The
third, a "new immanentism, " sees that the whole is
"determined not from outside but from within. "

Appearing as though in response to this inferred need
for a new guiding philosophy is a "New Age" paradigm,
dimly defined as yet but featuring a kind of ecological
consciousness that satisfies Ferkiss' three conditions.
It is characterized by (a) a metaphysic asserting transcendant man, and (b) the goal of a person-centered society. Whether this seemingly spontaneous emergence
of a new outlook is fortuitous coincidence or response
to a subliminally perceived need of society is a moot
but unimportant point. In either event, the coincidence
of the need and the emergence of a possible answer to
the need increases the likelihood that we are witnessing
the beginnings of a thoroughgoing paradigm shift.

The basic premises of the "New Age" paradigm are by
no means new. The belief in transcendant man, with
unlimited potentiality to comprehend the innermost
workings of his universe, to have immediate perception of a supersensible reality and of his intimate relationship with it, has been the esoteric tradition of
all the world's religions for thousands of years.[7] The

goal of a person-centered society was the foundation stone of this nation. "The Declaration (of Independence) put the individual squarely at the center, as of supreme importance. It completely reversed the age-old order; it defined government as the servant of the individual, not his master."[8] It would be the becoming dominant and operative of these premises and goals which would be new--which would comprise metanoia.

The 1960 report of the President's Commission on National Goals stated emphatically that "The paramount goal...is to guard the rights of the individual, to ensure his development, and to enlarge his opportunity.. All of our institutions--political, social, and economic-- must further enhance the dignity of the citizen, promote the maximum development of his capabilities, stimulate their responsible exercise, and widen the range and effectiveness of opportunities for individual choice... The first national goals to be pursued...should be the development of each individual to his fullest potential.. Self-fulfillment is placed at the summit(of the order of values). All other goods are relegated to lower orders of priority.. The central goal, therefore, should be a renewal of faith in the infinite value and the unlimited possibilities of individual development". What was not clearly understood in 1960 and is more apparent now, is that a fundamental incompatibility exists between these aims and the dominant paradigm of the industrial state.

III. Some specific implications for society

Thus we have argued that (a) the industrial era, which can be thought of as (in historical terms) a gigantic unprecedented step toward new possibilities for man, has been based in a paradigm which, however well suited to

that step, seems now fundamentally inappropriate to
the task of constructing a humane world on the base of
those technological accomplishments; and (b) a new
and suitable paradigm may be in process of replacing
the old. [9]

If this (admittedly) audacious and non-demonstrable)
proposition turns out to be accurate, and the claimant
"New Age" paradigm does become dominant, it will--
as we have noted--amount to a profound and pervasive
systemic change. All institutions of the society will
be affected.

The meaning of the metanoia can be better grasped if
we attempt to guess at likely changes in specific areas.
We do this, not as an attempt at prediction, but in the
endeavor to better understand what this change might
mean for the society.

Science. Science, in the claimant paradigm, will be
clearly understood to be a moral inquiry. That is to
say, it will deal with what is empirically found to be
good for man--in much the same sense that the science
of nutrition deals with what foods are wholesome for
man. It will place particular emphasis on the systematic exploration of subjective experience, the ultimate
source of our value postulates. In this respect, it will
resemble the humanities and religious, and the boundaries between these three disciplines will become
less sharp--as is already presaged in the recent writings of some psychotherapists. [10]

Applied science, particularly educational research,
will look strongly in the direction of new potentialities
suggested by the newly appreciated powers of belief,

imagination, and suggestion. To conscious choice and subconscious choice (repression, projection, sublimation, etc.) will be added what might be termed "supraconscious choice."[11] (intuition, creative imagination, choosing "better than we know")--with as much impact upon our policies regarding education, welfare, criminal rehabilitation, and justice as the Freudian concept of "subconscious choice"--e.g., repression, projection, sublimation, etc.--had some years earlier. Finally, the new science would become also a sort of "civil religion" supporting the value postulates of the Founding Fathers rather than being neutral or undermining as was the old science.

Institutions. Clearly the new metaphysic would tend to support effective institutionalization of such values as society serving the self-fulfillment of the individual, equality of justice before the law, individual fulfillment through community, human dignity and meaning, honesty and trust, self-determination for individuals and minority groups, and responsibility for humankind and the planet. However, values do not become operative simply by being deemed "good."

In general, the more significant a fraction of the whole is a subsystem, the more important it becomes that its goals be in close alignment with those of the overall system. It would be quite practical to foster (through changes in corporation, tax, and anti-trust laws, credit policies, special subsidies, etc.) the development of profitmaking corporations whose operative goals include active response to social problems (as of those of nonprofit corporations already do) and fostering the educational growth and development of all persons involved (as the goals of universities already do). In fact,

if something like this does not take place the amount
of government regulation required for pollution control, fair business and employment practice, resource conservation, etc. , can only increase without
limit.

In short, the institutionalization of the values of the
"person-centered society" would appear to be not only
morally desirable, but "good business" for the nation.

Economic system. The portion of the industrial-state
paradigm underlying the present operation of the economic system includes such concepts as man as infinite consumer of goods and services (providing his
appetites are properly whetted through advertising),
profit maximizing and economic growth as pre-eminent goals, and government as master regulator of
employment level, growth rate, wage and price stability, and a modicum of fair play. The new paradigm
would remind us that the root meaning of "economics"
is home management, and that the planet earth is man's
home. Managing the earth, with its finite supplies of
space and resources and its delicate ecological balance,
and conserving and developing it as a suitable habitat
for evolving man, is a far different task than that for
which the present economic system was set up.

Education. If the society does indeed undergo metanoia,
one of the most significant ways in which the transformation will be manifested will be in the premise that education is the paramount function of society. Robert Hutchins[12] describes "the learning society" as one that will
have transformed" its values in such a way that learning,
fulfillment, becoming human, and become its aims and
all its institutions were directed to this end. This is what

the Athenians did... They made their society one designed to bring all its members to the fullest development of their highest powers... Education was not a
segregated activity, conducted for certain hours, in
certain places, at a certain time of life... It was the
aim of the society.. The Athenian was educated by the
culture, by Paidea." And the central task of Paidea
was "the search for the Divine Center. "[13]

The individual will have several careers during his
lifetime. This is not because they are forced upon
him by job obsolescence in a technological-industrial
megamachine madly careening out of control and ever
faster. Rather, it will be because it is in this way that
he best realizes his own potentialities and maximizes
his own fulfillment. But this will require institutional
changes to accommodate to more or less continuous
education throughout life, with particularly intense
learning activity during periods of career change.

The precise way in which this will be resolved cannot
be foreseen, of course. Perhaps a multiplicity of institutional forms will be required, including new kinds
of collaborative arrangements between educational institutions and industrial and commercial organizations.
The emergence of new types of profit-making corporations with diversified goals, as suggested above,
might help to legitimate the growth-promoting and
educational activities which seem impracticable under
present laws affecting corporations.

It is along these lines that the society would approach the
"unneeded people" problem which was earlier identified
as one of the key ways in which the breakdown of the industrial-state paradigm is becoming manifest. The
"recycling" of those persons engaged in career change

will take the stigma off the recycling of those which the
modern industrial state shunts out of the productive
mainstream, usually irretrievably--those labeled
"technologically disemployed, "unemployable ," "dropout, " "poor, " "delinquent,'' "criminal, " "deviant, "
and "mentally ill. " Appropriate emotional support and
educational opportunity will be the assumed responsibility of widely distributed public, private, and voluntary organizations, rather than the charge of a huge
welfare bureaucracy which dispenses "income maintenance" but not human concern.

IV. The relevance to present decisionmaking

The intent of this paper is neither alarmist nor utopian,
but practical. All policy decisions are guided by some
interpretation of the past, and some vision of the future--
or of alternative futures.

A competing view would see neither necessity for, nor
evidence suggesting, such a basic paradigmatic change.
In this view the future would be approximated by a smooth
continuation of past trends. [14]

Two observations are crucial: (a) At this point in history
each of these two alternative views can be made plausible,
and each is held by many reasonable men. (b) The rational national policies which would be derived from the
two views differ greatly; some policies which seem sensible in one view appear harmful in the other.

Thus at the least, it would seem prudent to test policy
decisions both against the eventuality that the view presented here may prove accurate, and also against the
opposite eventuality, that it may simply turn out to be
wrong and our current travails will be interpreted in

some other way.

Under the assumption that the paradigm-shift interpretation is more or less correct (that is, that the shift seems possible and desirable, but by no means automatic), it follows that the main challenge to society is to bring about the transition without shaking itself apart in the process. Every major policy decision tends either to foster the change or to impede it. Actions which attempt to force it too fast can be socially disruptive; actions which attempt to force it back can make the transition more difficult and perhaps bloody. For example, there can be little doubt that maintenance of strong economic and legal-enforcement systems through the transition period is essential; yet these systems too must be flexible to change. Seldom in history has such delicacy of balance been required, to achieve a major social transformation rapidly and yet not rupture the social fabric.

Willis W. Harman is the Director of the Educational Policy Research Center, Stanford Research Institute.

Forecasting and Specifying Education Futures

Notes and References

1. Various reports of the Educational Policy Research
   Center, Stanford Research Institute including:
   Research Memorandum 6747-6, Alternative Futures
   and Educational Policy: February, 1970.
   Research Note 6747-11, Alternative Futures: Contexts
   in Which Social Indicators Must Work; February, 1971.
   Research Memorandum 6747-10, Projecting Whole-
   Body Future Patterns--The Field Anomaly Relaxation
   (FAR) Method; February, 1971.
2. Mumford, Lewis, The Transformation of Man, p. 231.
   Harper and Brother, New York; 1956.
3. The word has recently been used in this sense in Pearce,
   Joseph C. , The Crack in the Cosmic Egg. Julian Press,
   New York; 1971.
4. Kuhn, Thomas S. , The Structure of Scientific Revolution. University of Chicago Press; 1962. Further dis-
   cussion of the psychological threat involved in paradigm change may be found in Polanyi, M. , Personal
   Knowledge; Maslow, A. , The Psychology of Science;
   Matson, F. , The Broken Image, and Rokeach, M. , The
   Open and Closed Mind. These remarks are based on
   the more extensive analysis of contemporary revolutionary forces by Norman McEachron, A Contemporary Framework for Social Change, EPRC RN-12,
   June 1971.
5. Mumford, Lewis, The Pentagon of Power. Harcourt,
   Brace, Jovanovich, New York; 1970.
6. Ferkiss, Victor C. , Technological Man: The Myth and
   the Reality. George Braziller, New York; 1969.
7. Huxley, Aldous, The Perennial Philosophy. Harper
   and Brothers, New York; 1945.
8. Goals for Americans, pp. 1, 3, 53, 48, 57. Prentice
   Hall, Englewood Cliffs, N. J. 1960.
9. Platt, John R. , The Step to Man. John Wiley & Sons,
   New York; 1966.
10. To mention a few: Carl Jung, Erich Fromm, Rollo
    May, Ira Progoff, Carl Rogers, Roberto Assagioli,
    J. F. Bugental.

Part II

Notes and References (cont'd)

11. Pitirim Sorokin's study The Ways and Power of Love
     (Beacon Press, 1954) is a pioneering effort by a
     noted sociologist to initiate a systematic study of
     supraconscious processes.
12. Hutchins, Robert, The Learning Society, Praeger,
     New York: 1968.
13. Jaeger, Werner, Paidea: The Ideals of Greek Culture
     Basil Blackwell, Oxford Press, 1945.
14. The majority of future forecasts do not assume a
     paradigm change. One of the most comprehensive of
     these is Herman Kahn and Anthony Wiener, The Year
     2000: A Framework for Speculation. MacMillan, New
     York; 1967. One which appears to have an alarmingly
     high probability is Bertram Gross, "Friendly Fascism
     A Model for America," Social Policy, Nov-Dec. 1970,
     pp 44-52.

Specifications for
an Educational System of the Future

David J. Irvine

WHAT THE SYSTEM SHOULD BE ABLE TO DO

Restructuring the American educational enterprise
to meet the demands of the future involves not only
improving what exists but also creating new organizations and methods. Simply adjusting the educational system to meet new conditions is not sufficient.
Concerted efforts must be made to plan for the future.
But what kind of future? What kind of education?

Rather than try to predict what the educational system
of the future will be, one may take as an appropriate
starting point the specification of what the system should
be able to do. In this way alternative solutions are more
likely to be considered without focusing prematurely on
any given solution and thus becoming locked into it.

The remainder of this article is made up of a set of
suggested specifications of what the educational system
of the future should be able to accomplish. Following
each specification is a brief rationale upon which it
is based.

1. The educational system of the future must be able to
deal with large numbers of students. This requirement
needs no justification. The rapid increase in world and
national population is testimony enough. Advances in

medical science are likely to make us under-estimate, even today, the extent to which population growth will become a factor in educational planning of the future. Developing technical skills required in a modern society will require large proportions of the growing population to stay in school for longer periods of time, thus multiplying the effects of population growth.

2. The system must accommodate itself to new and different population patterns. The traditional boundaries between cities, suburbs, small towns, and rural area are rapidly being erased or rendered inappropriate to the realities of population concentrations. The residents of a suburb may have more at stake in the government of the city in which they work than in the town they live. Systems of government which integrate the interests of several municipalities may be required in the future. Educational systems will need to reflect this same trend.

Even state boundaries are becoming anachronisms. Washington, D. C. , now covers portions of Maryland and Virginia as well as the District of Columbia in everything but name and legal designations. Newark and New York City share airports and problems even though they lie in different states. What kind of governmental arrangement will be suitable for the megalopolis which will extend between Richmond and Boston by the year 2000? What kind of educational system will serve it?

In addition to these changes, population will most likely be concentrated in certain areas of the country. The population density of New York City will, in the future, be found in perhaps a dozen areas of the United States. Will then, the ills of education now apparent in New York City be visited upon these other areas? Or can we, by planning and ingenuity, anticipate the problems and solve them before they become all but insoluble?

3. The system must be capable of utilizing new technological developments for educational purposes. In order to cope with the greatly increased numbers of students, educational systems will need to find ways of bringing educational services to greater numbers of students without a proportional increase in manpower and money. Teaching machines and computer-assisted instruction are two examples of technology available today to multiply the effect of human teachers. Greater use of these developments as well as the creation of other innovations, will help stimulate greater learning among more students.

In addition to the pressures of large numbers of students, the rapidly rising cost of education demands attention. Education is one of the most highly labor-intensive industries. In the manufacturing industries higher wages have been justified largely by the greater productivity of workers. This increased productivity has been to a great extent due to the application of technology to manufacturing. There has been no parallel increase in productivity in the service industries such as education. Yet, in order to remain competitive, wages in these industries have risen in proportion to those in the manufacturing industries. If education is to increase productivity and thereby blunt the "taxpayers' revolt," it must seek ways to extend the impact of the individual teacher to greater numbers of students.

4. The system must capitalize on the many other educational forces which exist in society. Another stra-

tegy for increasing the productivity of educational organizations is to break down the artificial barriers between the institutions which we commonly identify as "educational" (for example, schools, libraries, museums, and colleges) and the many other repositories of information, skills, and processes within the community. Programs which use the total community, including the business community, rather than restrict themselves to the usual "educational" institutions, may provide many advantages, not the least of which is greater learning for the money.

5. The system must be able to bring learners in contact with a wide variety of realistic learning experiences. In spite of the many educational media now available, the bulk of learning is stimulated through the use of books, lectures, and rather simply conceived student-teacher interractions. The present calls for less reliance on such a narrow range of instructional approaches; the future will demand it. As we begin to apply more effectively what we know about human learning, we will utilize multisensory media which provide analogs to the real situations for which learners are being prepared.

6. The system must accommodate itself to changes in the natural resources available to man. Many natural resources which we have until recently taken for granted are being changed. The most notable of these are air and water. Sources of energy and raw materials may change in their availability, costs, and efficiency. As a result, man will need to learn new ways of utilizing his resources as well as new ways of adapting himself to the conditions which confront him. The educational system will be subject to these influences while it is developing adaptable learners.

7. The system must be capable of coping with increased amounts of information. The explosion of knowledge in almost every field of human endeavor requires that we develop ways of processing information so that it does not become unmanageable. Information systems are vulnerable to information overload. We can foresee the day when educational systems become so swamped with knowledge that students are exposed to confusing, perhaps almost random, bits of the total sum of knowledge. In addition, the very means of collecting, processing, storing, and disseminating information are likely to become clogged.

Organization of knowledge is becoming as important as facts. We cannot rely on each learner to supply his own organization. He must be taught how to organize his knowledge without being provided an inflexible organization which destroys creative thinking.

8. The system must be concerned with economy of learning. The increased amounts of information available and the accelerating change in the world will also require that a great deal of learning be squeezed into limited time. The student should not have to tolerate slow ways of teaching when faster and equally effective ways exist. Greater resourcefulness in integrating human and technological instructional capabilities will utilize human beings in those jobs they do best--synthesizing complex fields of information and feelings, for example--while freeing them from tasks at which they are relatively inefficient, such as storing and retrieving information.

9. The system must emphasize the development of learning skills. The two preceding specifications have brought into focus the problems of increasing amounts of infor-

mation. This characteristic of our time, plus the accelerating pace of change, will militate against the schools' being able to transmit all necessary learning.

Change is taking place at an accelerating pace, and the nature of change is changing. New knowledge does not merely pile onto old knowledge; it changes the old knowledge. Man's work changes not only because a machine now does his work faster and better, but also because machines are doing jobs which were not feasible using raw man-power. It is becoming less and less likely that the learning one goes through at one stage of his life will be completely adequate for a later stage. For this reason the individual must have the necessary learning skills available when he encounters learning situations throughout his lifetime.

10. The system should progressively involve the learner in making decisions about his educational program so that ultimately the learner controls his own learning. As learning becomes a lifelong process, the learner must have, in addition to learning skills, the ability to plan and decide on his own learning needs. An educational system which provides for decisions to be made for the learner without involving him in the decision-making process is likely to produce docile, indecisive individuals. The system of the future must help the individual learn to make decisions; the most obvious starting point is in his educational program.

11. The system must develop broadly educated specialists. The high level of technology which our society will attain in the next few decades will require technical training of many citizens. Decisions in business, education, and government will require both technical knowledge and a grasp of the "big picture." The size

of the population of the world, the complexity of the
world, the speed of communication, and the intricate
organizational patterns of our institutions will require
a broad education. The technician must be a "universal
man, " and leaders must know much technical detail
of the operations they command.

12. The system must emphasize human relations. In
a very real sense, modern communication and transportation are rapidly making us neighbors to people in
all parts of the world. Communication satellites have
illustrated dramatically the possibilities of instantan-
eous transmission of pictures, and sound. The "Town
Meeting of the World" is a reality.

Technical advances in transportation have brought us
in more rapid contact with other people. In addition,
more individuals now have the economic resources to
travel within their own countries and to other countries.

The increasing mobility of the population brings people
of diverse backgrounds together, and it brings more
people into already-congested areas. Crime in urban
areas is probably less a function of a "breakdown in law
and order" than it is a function of more people being in
contact with more people, geometrically increasing the
possibility of conflict.

13. The system must provide the means by which individuals can determine overriding purposes in their lives.
Many of the traditional influences which gave meaning to
our lives have lessened in their impact. Today we see
the influence of the family lessened by distance if not by
a changing defition of the concept of marriage. The church
is experiencing growing (or more accurately, shrinking)
pains. An individual's work may also come to direct his

life less, if shorter working hours and distance of
work from home are guides.

To remedy these losses in guidance, the individual
will have to depend more heavily on his own inner resources. His purposes in life will be more nearly a
product of his own efforts than it is of family, church,
or other traditional influences.

14. The system must help individuals break down the
dichotomy between work and play. In order to accomplish his life purposes, the educated person of the future will have to look at work and play as part of a
total plan: Work will be play in the sense that it is en-
joyable and challenging; play will be work in the sense
that it is meaningful rather than merely time consum-
ing.

Shortened work hours and increased leisure time must
be part of the individual's life plan. Escaping from work
merely to have more time to fill with entertaining is
neither constructive nor satisfying.

15. The system must help each individual, regardless of
characteristics and previous condition, to release the
potential he possesses. Society, that faceless monolith
which is really us, forces patterns of behavior which are
inimical to individual development. Discrimination,
whether it is based on race or on tradition, is still discrimination. The woman who causes raised eyebrows
by entering a male-dominated occupation is as surely the
victim of discrimination as is the black trying to enter a
white-dominated occupation; but society is also a victim,
since it may be deprived of the benefit of the woman's
and the black's best talents.

Forecasting and Specifying Education Futures

The system can help overcome discrimination by preparing individuals to realize their potential; but it must
also help by preparing society to accept the best of each
individual.

Man has been interested in the future ever since he has
been able to conceive of a time dimension. To dream of
the future is to extend history beyond the present.

However, modern man has moved beyond merely dream-
ing about the future. He predicts the future with a degree
of accuracy. He plans for the future. And by planning, and
acting upon his plans, he assists in fulfilling his predictions.

Shaping the future--or as Bennis has aptly phrased it,
"inventing relevant futures "[*]--may be the most important role for leaders of the educational enterprise during
the balance of this century. Imaginative planning and vi-
gorous action are imperative to maintain a viable educational system. The educational system of the future will
be shaped by men in purposive fashion, or it will, by de-
fault, be shaped by accident, tradition, and the senseless
forces of the environment.

David J. Irvine(663, University of North Carolina
Chapter) is chief of the Bureau of School Programs
Evaluation, New York State Education Department.

[*] Warren G. Bennis, "A Funny Thing Happened on the Way
to the Future," American Psychologist , July 1970
pp. 595-608.

What Will the Schools Become?

Harold G. Shane and Owen N. Nelson

IF THE FUTURE IS WHAT WE MAKE IT, AND SINCE
WE WILL ALL SPEND THE REST OF OUR LIVES
THERE, MUCH CAN BE SAID FOR THE CURRENT
INTEREST IN FUTURE-PEERING. HERE ARE THE
RESULTS OF THE PEERING OF 333 SCHOOL PERSONS
INTO SCHOOL PROBLEMS A QUARTER OF A CENTURY
HENCE. THE FINDINGS ARE ENCOURAGING.

Man has always had a keen interest in his future. In
the present climate of speculation, how does the U.S.
educator perceive our changing schools in the interval,
between 1975 and 2000? What does he believe may happen, when it is likely, and does he like what he anti-
cipates? What changes seem likely to come about
easily and where will the schools resist change most
vigorously?

In an effort to obtain thoughful conjectures about developments just over the horizon, the authors invited 570
persons[1] to react to 41 possible educational futures, all
of them discussed in more than 400 books and articles
dealing with alternatives for the next 30 years. Of the
respondents, 58% answered 205 queries which dealt
with 1) curriculum and instruction, 2) new organizational patterns and pupil policies, 3) economic and political
influences, 4) teacher preparation and status, 5) the
school's relationship to society, and 6) biological intervention and mediation tactics such as the use of drugs

to increase the children's teachability.

The responses reveal the status and direction of educators' thinking. They merit added consideration because of the "self-fulfilling prophecy" phenomenon, which suggests that the beliefs of our sample, if widely held, could perceptibly influence future developments in education. A few of the questions in all six areas have been selected for discussion here.

CURRICULUM AND INSTRUCTION

Multimedia. Almost all of the educators (93%) anticipate that a mix of learning resources will replace the traditional monopoly that the textbook has enjoyed as a mainstay of instruction. Virtually everyone (96%) agrees that a multimedia approach is desirable, that such approaches would be fairly easy to bring about, and that they will become prevalent between 1975 and 1985.

Student tutors. The use of student tutors (for example, 11 year-olds working with six-year olds in reading) will be commonplace if not a standard procedure by the early 1980's, in the opinion of almost three-quarters of the survey participants. Four out of five feel the idea is excellent, and two-thirds think it would be easy to start such programs.

A new English alphabet. The predictions and enthusiasm of a few linguists notwithstanding most respondents are pessimistic about the prospects for a phonetic alphabet of approximately 45 letters, which more nearly coincides with the number of phonemes (significant speech sound units) in English. While three out of four concede the

virtue of such a change, over half think it is unlikely
to be adopted and assign a low priority to the task.

Increased time for the expressive arts. Teachers of
drama, art, and music will be cheered to know that
over half of their fellow educators participating in the
survey are convinced that work in the expressive arts
will double its present time allotment in the curriculum
within 10 to 15 years. Seventy-five percent also believe
the 100% increase is desirable.

Controversial issues. An overwhelming 91% of the
educators feel that, before 1980, instruction in the
social studies will come to grips with controversial
topics (activist movements, discrimination, and so on),
and over 90% think that it is high time to give top priority of the forthright study of these social issues. Opinion is split as to how much public resistance there
might be to controversial content and issues on which
the schools took a stand.

With reference to sex education and despite the fact that
60% feel it would be difficult, 89% of the educators believe
that comprehensive study of human sexuality in all its
aspects should begin in the primary years. Four-fifths
urge that the introduction of sex education programs
receive high priority.

ORGANIZATION AND PUPIL POLICIES

A 12 month year and personalized programs. The organization of U.S. education and many of its long-familiar
policies are due to change sharply and rapidly if the
views of professors, teachers, and administrators are
accurate. No later than the mid-Eighties, 84% believe

our schools will be open for 12 months and students'
programs will be so personalized that the individual
can leave school for three months each year, choosing
both the time and the length of vacations. Educators
concede, however, that the public will be reluctant to
accept such flexibility. Noncompetitive "personalized
progress records" are endorsed, but a strong minority
(38%) foresee that grades will be used to report pupil
achievement for another 10 to 15 years.

Early childhood education. Respondents were optimistic when asked whether school services would extend downward to enroll three-year-olds and to provide health services for babies no later than at age 2.
Three-quarters of the replies favor such early childhood programs. Some 73% further urge that high priority be assigned to early childhood education and estimate that programs for the youngest will be a universal reality by around 1985. A large majority of
the sample is convinced that the British infant schools
will influence practice, and they believe this is a good
thing.

Revision of compulsory attendance laws. Opinions of
the survey population are almost evenly divided on
whether compulsory attendance laws will be relaxed,
although 63% favor the idea if exit from and reentry
into school can be made more socially acceptable, personal, and flexible. Attendance policies will be hard to
change, 60% said, although most feel that they ought
to be eased to permit students to leave school sooner
to enter the world of work.

FUNDING AND FINANCIAL POLICIES

Government agencies. The respondents forecast (62%)

and endorsed (88%) rapid consolidation of federal
education programs. Strong and united professional
action is required to accomplish this goal, and 82
out of 100 urge a high priority for coordinated action
by school officials. Even so, 10% of the respondents
conjecture that it will be the year 2000 before cooperation among governmental agencies replaces du-
plication and competititon. One extreme cynic cast
a write-in vote for 2500 A.D. as the probable year
of consolidation for overlapping agencies.

Differentiated staffing. Despite heated opinions on
differentiated staffing, 74% of the educators favor
differentiation with teacher-pupil ratios, but with
paraprofessionals and educational technology util-
ized to decrease teacher-pupil contact hours. This
is viewed as a means of increasing productivity, efficiency, and wages. Another large group, 66%, indicate that differentiated staffing probably will be
accepted, though not without a struggle. If the respondents' hunches prove accurate, a substantial
degree of differentiation will be attained within the
decade.

Performance contracting. The average respondent
is opposed to the idea of corporation management of
school systems, but feels there is an even chance it
will be more widely adopted. Estimates on when business may engage in increased school management res-
ponsibilities vary somewhat, but four out of five educators feel it could occur quickly. Ten percent believe
that the purchase of instruction from corporations will
be far more wide-spread as soon as four years from now

Vouchers for tuition payments. Little enthusiasm is

indicated for a voucher system. Seventy-one percent of the sample feel that such a plan will not get off the ground, and 67% condemn the idea. If vouchers ever are distributed, fewer than 15% see them coming into general use before 1985.

Salary and teacher performance. The antipathy toward merit rating which teachers have expressed for many years apparently has transferred to salary schedules based on teaching performance. Nearly 54% feel that performance-based wages and increments are not likely in the future. However, two-thirds of the replies acknowledged the desirability of basing salaries on competence.[2]

TEACHER PREPARATION AND STATUS

Teacher education and certification. Major changes in the preparation and licensing of teachers are widely accepted by those polled. For example, 92% feel that teacher education will be drastically modified to prepare pre-service students to work in teams or partnerships, to individualize instruction, to make use of educational technology, and to encourage greater pupil participation in the process of education. Routine use of sensitivity training in teacher education is foreseen by 64% of the respondents. Virtually all respondents (98%) favor major changes. There is also a pronounced feeling (82%) that alternatives to state-controlled teacher licensing are desirable, that they will be instituted (73%), and that they will be widely accpeted by 1980 or 1985.

A strong current of opinion suggests that ways of obtaining teaching certificates should be liberalized(67% said "yes") and that few if any of the new avenues

should involve merely adding courses in professional
education. Major changes are presumably to be in-
augurated in the immediate future and, for the most
part, completed in 10 to 15 years.

The self-contained classroom. "One teacher-one
group" instruction is on the way out, according to
69% of the respondents predicting the shape of the
future. Another larger group (75%) apparently say
"good riddance" to this venerable institution.

In place of the self-contained classroom, 67% of the
educators see (and 79% cheerfully accept) some form
of "flexible teaching partnerships ." Presumably,
such partnerships would be an extension of the team
concept, but would involve greater "horizontal" and
"vertical" deployment of a differentiated staff; that
is, a given teacher would work "vertically" with
more children of different ages and "horizontally"
in more varied capacities.

THE SCHOOL AND SOCIETY

Societal services. The school is viewed as an agency
responsive to social change by most of the participants.
Judging by majority opinions of social engineering, we
can anticipate 1) psychiatric treatment without cost to
students (76% said "yes, " 87% "desirable"), [3] 2)massive
adult education and vocational retraining programs (92%
said "yes, " 95% "desirable"), and 3) school programs
designed to help adults adjust to increased leisure and
longer periods of retirement (85% said "yes, " 94% "desirable").

Mandatory foster homes. Respondents were asked

whether they thought that children, before age three, might be placed in foster homes or kibbutz-type boarding schools to protect them from a damaging home environment. Opinions are about evenly divided on whether this is a good or bad policy, but the likelihood of such a development in the U.S. is rejected by over 70%.

INTERVENTION AND MEDIATION

One of the more controversial items among the 41 in the educational futures instrument is whether or not, in the years ahead, schools should and will use chemical compounds to improve the mood, memory, power of concentration, and possibly the general intelligence of the learner. Most of the respondents feel that what is measured as intelligence can be increased substantially. Ninety percent of the survey participants consider it appropriate to try to increase the IQ through such mediation tactics as enriched environment in early childhood, and 82% also express confidence that measurable intelligence will be increased by or before 1990.

However, the use of drugs to increase "teachability" was labeled as both unlikely (57% say it will not occur on a widespread scale) and a bad practice to boot. Fifty-six percent rejected the idea of using stimulants, tranquilizers, or antidepressants.

"Intervention" in early childhood. The presumed importance of education under school auspices in the learner's early years is supported by survey respondents. Over 70% feel that "preventive and corrective intervention" before age six might, within the next 25 years, make the annual per pupil expenditures for the early-childhood

Part II

group even higher than per-student costs are at the
university level.

CONCLUSION

Our small sample--directly or by implication--ex-
presses great confidence in the influence of and financial support for education between 1975 and 2000.
The respondents expect and desire substantial educational changes; their dissatisfaction with the status
quo comes through clearly. If the 333 respondents who
struggled patiently through the survey instrument
represent U.S. educators as a whole, then the coming
decade should attain levels of humaneness and educational zest and venturesomeness reminiscent of the
1930's, the heyday of the progressive education movement.

Harold G. Shane (2650, Indiana University Chapter) is
University Professor of Education at Indiana University,
and Owen N. Nelson (114, La Crosse Wisconsin Field
Chapter) is assistant professor of education at Wisconsin
State University.

NOTES AND REFERENCES

1. Respondents were selected from among five occupa-
tional categories: school administrators (72), subject
matter specialist (42), curriculum professors(37), doc-
toral students (87), and a random sample of public
school teachers (95).
2. This does not necessarily accurately reflect classroom
teachers' attitudes. Only 95 of the 333 were teachers.
3. Most (76%) of the educators expect public schools to
assume routine responsibility for identifying and treating
incipient mental and psychological disorders in childhood
89% favor the idea.

Changing Influences
in American Education

"THE CONCEPT OF THE MONOLITHIC PUBLIC
DEMOCRATIC SCHOOL SERVED AN IMPORTANT
PURPOSE IN THE EARLY DECADES OF THIS
CENTURY...BUT A MONOLITHIC STRUCTURE
IS VERY UNREAL IN THE KIND OF SOCIETY WE
SEEM TO BE DEVELOPING NOW."

Wilbur J. Cohen

A Gallup Poll published early in 1972 showed that 28
percent of persons surveyed in the United States were
dissatisfied with their children's education. This figure compared with the 54 percent dissatisfied with
their work. The dissatisfaction with education was
approximately the same as dissatisfaction with the
individual's housing situation (23%), and the family's
future (30%). The proportion that were satisfied with
their children's education, however, was 60 percent,
with 12 percent having no opinion.

A 1971 survey of teachers by the National Education
Association showed that not quite 5 in 10 thought teaching as a profession was getting better; 4 in 10
thought it was getting worse, and 1 in 10 thought that
the profession was staying about the same as before.
As school-system size increased, there was a corresponding increase in the percentage of teachers who
thought that teaching as a profession was getting worse.

Reprinted with the copyright permission of Current
History, Inc., August, 1972.

These expressions of divergent views about education among parents and teachers could be shown to
exist among students as well. At the same time, the
taxpayer has expressed his strong support for education by increasing the proportion of the gross national product devoted to all levels of education public and private) from about 4 percent in 1950 to 5
percent by the mid-1960's, 6 percent by 1968, and
close of 7 percent at the present time. This is a
striking increase, although it is not clear whether
this financial support is reluctant or enthusiastic.

Education is a large and growing enterprise in the
American economy: it involves, at all levels, some
3.25 million teachers and staff in schools, some
60 million students, and over 125,000 board members. It is largely a "socialized" enterprise, involving about five percent of the nation's labor force
employed by governmental agencies on a salary
basis, with the facilities owned and operated by governmental agencies. But private nonprofit agencies
play a very significant role in educational operations
and policy, while private profit-making enterprises
in book and magazine publishing, audio-visual and
media equipment and materials, and research and
evaluation play an important part in the development
and dissemination of materials and aids to teachers,
students and institutions.

So many changes have been taking place in education
and society recently that it is not possible to portray
comprehensively what these changes are, or how they
affect all the participants in the system, much less to
identify, with precision, the implications for the future.

The very nature of education makes it subject to change over time and the rapid process of economic, social and scientific developments in recent years has affected educational policy and practice. At the same time, there are some common and persistent elements in educational goals. Each generation and each period of historical change tend to pour the educational wine into different educational bottles, and then carefully save the bottles so that another generation may pour the wine back into them. The methods of pouring the wine back and forth change, but the bottles change very little.

In one sense, there is nothing basically very new in all the recent proposals for educational change. In one way or another, most so-called "innovations" probably have been tried or proposed somewhere or sometime before. And, by various criteria, most educational innovations turn out to be, at best, partially successful, and partially unsuccessful. The proportion of success may vary from time to time or place to place.

TEN AREAS OF CHANGE

A full listing of the many changes under way in American education would require several volumes. A selected list of ten areas of change is only an indication of less than one-tenth of the iceberg floating on the educational seas. In the following discussion, ten factors are outlined which m ay play a part in changing the educational system, the society, and the way in which our children and grandchildren may function in the remaining three decades of this century.

1. Changes in Financing School Expenditures. The current criticism of the local residential property tax as an unsatisfactory method of financing elementary and

secondary education is very likely to result in a number of changes affecting not only the financing but the control and leadership of education. The property tax is an inflexible and unprogressive method of meeting the needs of a dynamic and growing society. Many local millage increases for school financing have been defeated in recent years. This has happened in wealthy communities, in middle-income communities, and in poor communities. We have failed to realize that we now have a larger proportion of older persons on fixed incomes. More and more of these older people, when confronted with a vote for an increased property tax on their homes, realize that they are voting for a reduction in their standard of living. Since they are on fixed incomes, whether social security or a private pension, they have no immediate way to get the increased income to pay the property tax.

Our population is getting older. In 1930, less than 6 percent of the population of the United States was over age 65; 10 percent now is, and the figure is going up. It stands to reason that the property tax is no longer a sound basis on which to obtain the amount of money we require to run an educational system that is consistent with our ideals and needs.

As state and federal governments assume a larger portion of the cost of education, they will undoubtedly also play a larger role in policy and leadership. The old stereotype of "local control" of education may give way to a new partnership between the three levels of government, parents, and students; a partnership which may be forged amidst much pain and suffering. Despite the stresses and strains in the financing of education in recent years, the fact is that the people of the United States have been contributing more for education, in

both absolute and relative terms, than they have in any
other period in our history, and it is likely that this
trend will continue in the coming decade.

2. Early childhood Education. For a long time schools
looked upon programs for children under age five as
babysitting or day-care custodial operations. The des-
perate need for funds in the regular elementary and secondary public schools precluded any substantial local
or state financial aid for preschool operations. As a
result, voluntary and profit-making enterprises took
the leadership in this area away from the public school
system. The recent surge of interest in the potentialities of preserving and enhancing the creativity, motivation and learning capacity among very young children
has been phenomenal. Its possible impact on children,
parents and the school system is unclear, but there is a
belief and a hope that it can and will be substantial. The
likelihood that this area will be financed almost wholly
by the federal government has many ramifications.

It is also clear that we must not become tied to just
"one" system of providing early childhood education.
There are many different alternatives which should
continue to be explored. Various programs could be
built on different theoretical bases. These include, for
example, a cognitive-oriented curriculum, an academically oriented program, or the Montessori system.
There is no doubt that with different emphases programs
should and will be developed in this crucial area. Nor
should we become tied to any "fixed" idea of what early
childhood education involves in terms of formal organization. In some areas, the need may be met by developing formal child-care centers; in other areas, perhaps,
the emphasis should be upon training an adequate supply
of paraprofessional and minority personnel who will

provide family care in their own homes. We should
try to establish a choice of facilities and services
in which parents may enroll their children. The diversity which characterizes our society should be
and probably will be reflected in the evolution of
early childhood education.

3. Desegregation, Busing and Quality Education. The
heated controversies over de jure and de facto segregation in schools and neighborhoods, and the intense flare-ups and political frustrations over busing
to redress segregation, all seem to point in one direction: the vital necessity of improving schooling.
The emotional issue of busing must inevitably be
viewed in the larger context of the practical alternatives necessary to improve the quality of education.

Busing is neither a panacea for all the ills which currently beset education, nor is it per se an evil to be
avoided at all costs. It can help and it has helped, to
improve the quality of education. On the other hand,
if prejudice, hostility and failure to improve the quality of education exist and persist in a local-area,
busing by itself will not resolve the difficulty, but
may intensify it. Consequently, busing must be viewed
as one possible method of dealing with some of the
problems of education at the local level, but not the
only, or even the primary, method of overcoming
these problems.

It is unrealistic to advocate a uniform federal policy,
which denies to a local school district or to the courts
the opportunity to utilize busing to meet the needs of
that particular situation. The recent debate on busing
has served to obfuscate one of the greatest problems

facing our society: the isolation of groups within our
society with a resultant harvest of fear, ignorance,
and lack of concern. Any educational policy which
has as its aim the maintenance of barriers to understanding and which forecloses opportunities to perceive the diversity which has given such strength to
our society is invalid for our day and age.

A quality education is not one that involves just the
traditional "three R's." Our children are growing
up in a complex world filled with great diversity of
cultures. They must be prepared, in their schooling,
to function successfully in this ever-changing world.

4. Collective Bargaining. The role of collective bargaining in the educational system has many obvious,
as well as subtle, reverberations on educational policies and practices. There is every indication that
the extent and importance of collective bargaining
will increase. And there is a likelihood that collective
bargaining will move from the local area to the statewide level.

Accompanying this broadening of operations, various
teacher unions and associations may merge to secure
a united organization in negotiating with their employers. And, as collective bargaining moves beyond the
local area, there will be great efforts made to secure
uniformity of pay-scales and benefits for employees
in the educational field. This would certainly have an
effect upon the methods by which school districts raise
the money to pay their employees. The possibility that
school administration will be decentralized, that some
children will be bused out of their home areas, and
that teachers will be hired from hitherto under-repre-

sented minority groups, may also have an impact on
the scope of collective bargaining and the way in which
the school system functions.

The unions and educational associations have also indicated a willingness to enter into another area which
has, until now, been unorganized: the realm of higher
education. We are currently witnessing an effot to organize university faculty and staff, and this process
shows signs that it will continue in the coming decade.
This could produce significant changes in the organization and management of our universities and colleges. The notion of a university existing as a "community of scholars" may undergo some changes if
the relationship between faculty and administration
is on more of an employee-employer basis. How this
will affect the entire educational system, including
the training of teachers, will warrant careful study.

5. Substitutions for Teacher Certification. Increasing
dissatisfaction with course-credit credentials for
certifying teachers has resulted in proposals for performance or competency-based teacher certification.
This goal is still far from being realized, but the next
few years will see great efforts made to develop objective criteria for evaluating the quality of teacher
performance.

The movement for periodic re-examination of comp-
etency which has been most pronounced recently in
medical care, will affect education as well as other
professional fields. The long-run implications of comp-
etency evaluation coupled with collective bargaining
and additional funds for education could be profound.
These factors could have a great impact on the content
of teacher education. It seems likely that more prac-

tice-teaching, coupled with increased supervision, may
be among the requirements for teacher education in the
future. Schools of education may have to reexamine their
curriculum and training programs periodically to insure
that those who are certified have the qualities necessary
for competent teaching in a rapidly changing world. We
shall, no doubt, see even greater emphasis placed upon
a variety of approaches, emphases and experiences at
all levels of education as a result of interest in a multi-
ethnic approach to education.

6. Innovation and Experimentation. The radically changing values in our society, the increased tempo of scientific and technological change, the new and varied life
styles that are evolving, and the greater leisure and the
discretionary incomes which are developing are all
factors affecting educational change. Who knows what
the economy and environment will be in the year 2010
when the current six-year-olds entering school will be
the parents and voters in the society of the next century.
With new or different perspectives on life styles and conduct, perhaps some of the old forms of instruction will
take on new value. A voucher system that is unaccept-
able while segregation and church-run schools exist may
be acceptable under different circumstances or at another moment. Compulsory education, so necessary at
one stage of history, may be repealed in part or may
give way to other laws affecting the education of parents
as well as students at another time. The 180-day school
year may be replaced by other schedules which might
utilize the available facilities more efficiently. Students
may move in and out of the educational system over a
period of time.

In his provocative book, FUTURE SHOCK,[1] Alvin Toffler
suggests that curriculum requirements must be justified

in terms of the future:

> Should all children be required to study algebra?
> Might they not benefit more from studying proba-
> bility? Logic? Computer programming? Philo-
> sophy? Aesthetics? Mass Communications?....
> Why, for example, must teaching be organized
> around such fixed disciplines as English, econo-
> mics, mathematics or biology? Why not around
> stages of the human life cycle: a course on birth,
> childhood, adolescence, marriage, career, re-
> tirement, death? Or around contemporary social
> problems? Or around significant technologies
> of the past and future? Or around countless other
> imaginable alternatives?

We should create the means in our educational establishment to explore some of these "countless other
imaginable alternatives." Sometimes the "outrageous"
alternative of one period becomes the "inevitable" of
another. There have been suggestions that in each
community we develop some schools with widely different approaches in the curriculum and give parents
and students an option as to which school and curriculum they wish to select. Our public school system
should and could provide more choices and options.
The concept of the monolithic public democratic school
served an important purpose in the early decades of
this century in drawing together the citizens of this
country, but a monolithic structure is very unreal in
the kind of society that respects variations in human
personality and recognizes differing levels of aspira-
tion may well try to develop many different kinds of
schools.

7. Teacher Shortage and Teacher Surplus. The teacher shortage of the 1950's has turned into a teacher

surplus in the 1970's. The challenge now is that schools
of education can turn more of their resources from the
demand for quantity to the urgent need for quality. But
the task is not a simple one, nor is it easily achieved.
It will mean substantially increased salaries for teachers   in relation to salaries for other comparable work.
It should mean more men in elementary education. The
possibility of developing teachers, researchers, administrators   and paraprofessional aides for early childhood education will place a new responsibility on teacher   training. And schools of education will have to
revise their programs to recruit more teachers for minority groups, the disadvantaged, the gifted and other
special needs. Schools of education will also be charged
with the responsibility of developing educational programs to facilitate the acquisition of skills and the renewal of knowledge by teachers already in the system.

If we expand our early childhood education programs
dramatically, the demand for teachers in this area
would shift immediately from the surplus that exists
at the present time to a vast shortage. The desirable
ratio of teachers to students in the early childhood
period is in the range of one to five or six, as compared to one to twenty-five or one to thirty in the existing elementary and secondary school systems. The
demand for teachers in early childhood education programs may result in increases in salaries in the elementary and secondary teaching area, which would have
a bearing on the financing of education.

The area of continuing education could encompass a
far larger percentage of the population than has previously been the case. We might see the integration
of previously small and isolated adult education and
continuing education programs into the mainstream

of academic life as interest in lifetime learning ex-
pands. When the idea that education does not end at
age 21 or 25 is universally accepted, the implementation of lifetime learning could revolutionize both
education and society.

8. Parent Involvement and Student   Participation.
Recent developments indicate that some parents and
students believe they can and should play a more
effective role in the educational   process. Parent
involvement in the professional and policy aspects
of education is likely to have substantial implications
for school boards, administrators, teachers and
students. The next decade may see a renewed interest in facilitating communication between those
charged with the responsibility of educating the child
and that child's parents.

There is a great likelihood that significant developments in making pre- and post-natal child care universally available will take place within the next
decade. It is conceivable that one thrust of expanded
early childhood education and health services may be
in the direction of educating the parents of a child
even before that child enters into the formal school
system. Because of the small number of professionals now working in this area, and because of the un-
even distribution of such professionals in the country the implementation of such program would have
to rely upon a large degree of parental involvement
and training.

The changing life styles of students and parents have
played a significant role in changing the tone and emphasis in schools and in educational programs. Dress,
discipline and other areas of conduct are changing.

It is not yet clear where all this will lead or what its results will be. But change is likely to be profound and pervasive.

9. Expectations from Education. Over the past 150 years the American people have come to expect and believe that education is "the" answer to any and all problems. Education has helped to improve economic conditions, reduce poverty, increase incomes, and expand science and technology. A substantial proportion of the body politic places major reliance on education for the improvement of conditions for citizens and their children. On the other hand, there is deep dissatisfaction among many young people, and some in other age groups, with conventional schooling, with the kind of world produced by the "educated" elite. The extent of alienation and frustration in our society reflects a dissatisfaction with the aims as well as the accomplishments of education.

NEED FOR PLURALISM?

Where these conflicting tendencies will lead us by the end of the decade is still unclear. As the values upon which our philosophy of education are challenged and contradicted, the need for a more pluralistic system of education may become ever more apparent.

10. Changing Community Institutions. Every teacher is aware of how much learning goes on outside of the school. It is clear that the school controls only part of the learning environment. What will be the effect on learning and schools if during this decade the nation adopts and puts into effect a program which eliminates discrimination on the basis of race, sex,

creed and national origin, abolishes poverty, estab-
lishes a minimum income for all, provides a reasonable floor of protection for every retired person, eliminates hunger and malnutrition, and provides a national health insurance system for everyone from birth to death? It would make some difference, but we will not really know how much it
affects education or other institutions until it happens.

Attitudes with respect to the role of men, women,
children, the family and school are undergoing
change. So are attitudes toward work, leisure and
what we think makes up "the quality of life. " Our
society is utilizing only a fraction of the energy,
creative ability, ideas and productivity of many wom-
en and some men. We are probably utilizing only
a fraction of the talent of most individuals. We know
that every major period of great torment and distress has resulted in new tools and approaches in
dealing with evolving problems. And among these
new developments there will be many that we will
not understand and many that we will not like.

We can, however, expect one certain development:
there will be unexpected ramifications and implications. The human brain and the human nervous system are so complex that we cannot yet fathom all
the possible lines of reaction to changing institutional
and personal roles. It appears that many changes
are in the making for our educational institutions
and programs.

CONCLUDING OBSERVATIONS

Education is viewed from many different perspectives by different audiences in the educational arena,

as for instance: students (at different age levels);
parents(in various socio-economic classes);
teachers (by size and location of school); taxpayers (in relation to the property tax); educators
(depending on their academic specialization); and
federal, state, and local legislators (depending
on their political outlook and geographical location). There are also other forces at work in mold-
ing these perspectives: religion, race, ethnic
background, and attitudes toward discipline, work,
roles of men and women and outlook on the world.
As all these forces change, so does education.

One of the major tasks of any educational system
should be the cultivation of diverse approaches to
the solution of social problems. We have enough
experience to know that there are no simple solutions to the many different problems that beset us.
A plea for diversity is not a request for chaos. It
is a recognition of the fact that when people have
the opportunity to make reasoned choices about
their lives, and the lives of their children, the value
of any decision that they make is greatly enhanced. If choice is limited, and knowledge is
conceived of as something fixed or absolute, then
any sort of social progress is marginal.

The frustrations of the teacher and administrator
in education are painful because the gap between
expectation and reality is so personal. The child
is here and now, and passes this way but once.
The teacher and parent can see the unlimited opportunities for the child, as well as the failures
in accomplishing them. The process of education
goes on for each child in each generation and

in each society amidst a changing environment, goals and priorities.

Wilbur J. Cohen was Secretary of Health, Education, and Welfare (1968-1969), having served as Assistant Secretary (1961-1965), and Under Secretary to John Gardner (1965-1968). Mr. Cohen was responsible for piloting some 40 education bills through Congress during the 1960's. He now serves as Dean of the School of Education, University of Michigan.

Notes and References

1. New York: Random House, 1970.

Education in 1980:
eight ways it will be different

Clark C. Abt

WE MAY EXPECT A GREATER DIVERSITY AND
CONFLICT AMONG EDUCATIONAL PHILOSOPHIES
AS RADICALS COMPETE WITH RADICALS TO BE
THE MOST RADICAL IN THE MOST NOVEL WAY...
AS CONSERVATIVES CONFLICT WITH CONSER-
VATIVES OVER WHETHER TO BE PRUDENTLY
MODERATE OR REACTIONARY.....AND AS
MODERATES AND LIBERALS SEEK TO REUNIFY
THESE DIVERGENT FACTIONS FOR THE GREATEST
GOOD FOR THE GREATEST NUMBER.

Few people would ever use the crystal ball on education, and there are good reasons why: the sticky financial situation, the various forces pulling against each
other on educational methods, plans and interests,
and the not-always-clear impact of new ideas. Still,
it is useful to pinpoint a number of trends which will
most likely occur in the next 10 years.

These major changes can be foreseen:

1. Preschool and post-graduate phases of education
will substantially expand. In addition, the relative
amount of formal public education will decline as professional, technical and educational recreation training increases.

2. In education technology, there will be a major shift
in emphasis from hardware and associated software

to what might be called behavioral technics. As
urban fiscal crises pinch available municipal funds,
school budget increases will be subject to the prior
claims of increasingly militant teacher unions and
the irrefutable demand for more schools imposed
by population growth. Very little extra money seems
likely to be available for new instructional hardware
or software that costs more than a few cents per
student per year.

The combination of these cost constraints, the demand for community control and decentralization
of schools, and the reform movements seeking to
break the public monopoly on education and introduce
a market mechanism which will offer incentives to
improvement, will provide a greater market for behavioral and organizational education inventions.

3. Informal education will become increasingly popular as an alternative to formal education for both
school-age youth and adults. The increasing availability of low-cost electronic communications, tape
recorders, film and videotape will make education
just as feasible and a lot more attractive in homes,
where students can proceed at their own pace.

On the other hand, particularly in view of the economic
squeeze affecting education hardware and software,
school activities will tend to change to more interper-
sonal, interactive discussions, team competitions,
and group problem-solving that can be conveniently
carried out in the home.

4. Education will be increasingly tied into recreation,
particularly on vacations. A large number of educated
active, young and middle-aged people will seek to com-

bine brief and intensive re-educational experiences with their vacations. For example, two weeks of doing nothing but lying on the beach, skiing or swimming at a mountain lake can lead to boredom. These people may be in the market for the same recreational activities, in the same pleasant setting, but combined with short and intensive courses in a variety of professionally relevant or esthetically satisfying fields--drawing, piano playing, sculpting, flying, welding, social science, research methods, house construction, masonry, architecture, graphic design, sensitivity training and group psychotheraphy, fiction writing, statistics, computer programming, yoga, political analysis, etc.

5. Technical and professional training will enjoy the largest absolute and percentage growth in investment probably growing from the current level of approx-imately $18 billion in the U. S. to at least three times that figure by 1980. The forces driving this enormous expansion are: the accelerated rate of technical change requiring retraining in operations and applications; the increase per capita productivity, yielding a greater surplus for reinvestment in human capital development; the increasing competitiveness of in-dustries for high-quality, problem-solving person-nel and the increasing complexity and rate of social and technical change of the society as a whole, which will require much greater specialization and continuous upgrading of R & D, production, marketing, finance, legal and general management activities.

6. The still strong "credentials" barrier will be gradually eroded by increasing pressures for greater participation in education and educational decision-

making by more non-professional community groups and individuals. Pressures generated by increased teacher unionization and higher budgets will lead administrators to seek additional instructional re- sources in paraprofessionals, teacher-students, and home auto-instruction.

7. A new type of educator will emerge who is specif- ically interested in the continuous improvement, rather than the orderly maintenance of educational systems. This new educator will have elements of the entrepreneur, the systems analyst, the behavior- ist, and the environmentalist. He will be relatively impatient with pure administration and will measure his own success in terms of the increase in the rate of learning gains achieved by a great diversity of stu- dent populations in subjects chosen by the students themselves.

In short, he will be something of a combination behav- ioral scientist and management efficiency expert. Training programs for this type of educator do not exist presently, but such people continue to appear in increasing numbers as a result of the demand for their capabilities and the increasing possibilities for interdisciplinary social research.

8. The next decade will see a great disorder and frag- mentation of education philosophies and doctrines anal- ogous to the ideological and socio-economical, gener- ational, and sexual polarizations of today. We may ex- pect a greater diversity and conflict among educational philosophies as radicals compete with radicals to be the most radical in the most novel way... as conserva- tives conflict with conservatives over whether to be

prudently moderate or reactionary...and as moderates and liberals seek to reunify these divergent factions for the greatest good of the greatest number.

This fragmentation may, hopefully, liberate the practical development of better instructional technics, materials and educational environmental management from the rigidity imposed by past doctrines.

Dr. Abt is president and founder of Abt Associates, Inc., Cambridge, Mass., an education consulting firm, and also a consultant to the Department of Health, Education and Welfare. This forecast for education is based on a number of government-sponsored policy studies.

The Future of Teacher Education

S. C. T. Clarke and H. T. Coutts

TEACHER EDUCATION WILL BE THE RESPON-
SIBILITY OF UNIVERSITIES... CANDIDATES WILL
BE REQUIRED TO EXHIBIT... EXCELLENCE IN
HUMAN RELATIONS AND ENGLISH USAGE... COM-
MON LEARNINGS REQUIRED OF ALL TEACHERS
WILL INCLUDE PREPARATION IN THE USE OF THE
LATEST EDUCATIONAL TECHNOLOGY AND MEDIA.

FUTUROLOGY

At an International Conference on Future Research
held at Kyoto, Japan, in April, 1970, almost every
aspect of futurology was explored. The scope was
broad. A quick glance at the titles of the papers presented indicates that the technological future based
on developments in physics, chemistry, biology, gen-
etics, and other sciences is almost sure to affect
the social future. It is in the context of technological
and social change that education in the future will be
set. Of the eight divisions of this conference, one
was devoted to the future of education.

A European planning group also sets education in a
wider context:

Plan Europe 2000 (12) groups, together for research
programmes whose common objective is to endeavor
by systematic thinking, to conceive of society as it

will be in the 21st century and the type of man capable
of regulating it. The projects relate to education, the
development of industrialization, urban development,
and rural development.

On this continent, the Institute for the Future, in con-
centrating on long-range forecasting of technological
and societal events, includes education among the latter. In the table of contents, one of its publications
lists under Future Developments (8).

1. Urbanization
2. The Family
3. Leisure and the Economy
4. Education
5. Food and Population
6. International Relations
7. Conflict in Society: Law Enforcement
8. National Political Structure
9. Values
10. Impact of Technology on Government and Society

There are two institutions in North America whose chief
function is to study the future of education, the Educational
Policy Research Center at Syracuse and the Educational
Policy Research Center at the Stanford Research Institute.
The Syracuse Center has stated (23);

Planning, whether in or outside of the educational system,
is an attempt to gain some control over the future, to reduce the intrinsic uncertainty of the future to manageable
proportions.

The Stanford Center has defined its function as follows (11):

The task of the Educational Policy Research Center is to illuminate the nature of basic issues, conceptualize possible alternative futures, and analyze the means available for the achievement of policy goals and the consequences of alternate choices.

Each of these centers has a list of publications on the future of education. A recent review of the literature (10) devoted 34 of the 331 multilithed pages to the future of education. This review was the starting point for the statements on education in the future used in the present study.

REVIEW OF PREVIOUS STUDIES

Although two institutions in the United States focus on the future of education, which has been studied as one part of futurology, the authors know of no study devoted specifically to the future of teacher education.

The elementary teacher education models sponsored by the United States Office of Education have been summarized and reviewed in the JOURNAL OF RE-SEARCH AND DEVELOPMENT IN EDUCATION[1] by Burdin (1), Clarke (4), Le Baron (15), Klatt and Le Baron (14), and a number of other authors. At least one of these models (20) attempted to look ten years ahead in teacher education. Its rationale included three phases: predictions for society by 1978 (e. g., the trend towards urbanization will be accelerated), predictions for education by 1978 (e.g., society will make increased demands upon schools and colleges to fashion programs to meet the needs of all of its people), and inferences about elementary school teaching by 1978 (e. g., only broadly educated persons of high ability will be able to make the difficult decisions required of elementary school teachers). This sequence (the anticipated future state of the world; the nation; education; teaching; the teaching profession, and therefore, teacher education) formed the basis for a task analysis of teaching in 1978 and of the preparation required. To a greater or lesser extent, each of the models adopted it, varying only in what has been called "extent of lead" (2), that is, the remoteness of the anticipated future.

Phase II of the USOE Elementary Teacher Education Models elicited some detailed reviews of studies of the future and of proposals to continue and extend such studies. Thus, Michigan State University (17) deveoted a 37 page chapter to systematic analysis of future society; items 3 and 4 in the "Statements About Education in the Future"[2] used in the present study derive from this source. The Syracuse University Phase II proposal (22) devotes a 10-page chapter, entitled "Scenario, " to a hypothetical exchange of correspondence between the program director and a student who, in 1977, is writing a history of the project. The Oregon College of Education Phase II proposal (19) provides societal and educational projections with relevant analysis and implications.

Teacher education for the future is the topic of a book in the seven-volume series of the eight-state project, DESIGNING EDUCATION FOR THE FUTURE; Volume 7 (18) is on teacher education. Each of its thirteen chapters is written by an expert on one aspect of teacher preparation. The flavor of the volume is indicated by the following quotation:

Training in self-consciousness and self-awareness;

in the capacity to absorb criticism without fear of
loss of esteem or worthiness; in a sensitivity to how
they are being perceived by their students and a
caring how they are perceived--these are some of
the new facets of teacher preparation that are required (18:17).

Two other sources of statements about teacher education in the future might be mentioned in passing.
In May 1970, Coutts presented an unpublished paper
on "Preparing the Teachers We Need." Also in 1970,
Clarke prepared a position paper for the Commission
on Educational Planning of the Province of Alberta
on teacher education in the year 2000.

The picture of teacher education in the future that
emerges from the studies reviewed is fragmentary
and incomplete; in many instances it derives from
the vision of one person. The present study sought
a consensus of expert opinion on the topic.

THE DELPHI TECHNIQUE

Weaver (21) presents a review of the Delphi forecasting method and concludes that it holds considerable promise as a pedagogical tool to be used to get
educators to think in more complex ways about the
future. Cyphert and Gant (6, 7) describe its use in
deriving statements about the goals of teacher education for a particular institution.

The basic features of the Delphi technique are (1)
anonymity for panelists during the forecasting (2)
controlled feedback to the panelists of opinions
generated in the several rounds of mailed interaction,
and (3) statistically descriptive group responses. The

technique originated in 1953 as an alternative to the traditional round-table discussion by experts. Advantages claimed for this approach are the elimination of:

...committee activity altogether, thus further reducing the influence of certain psychological factors, such as specious persuasion, the unwillingness to abandon publicly expressed opinions, and the bandwagon effect of majority opinion (13).

Within the broad framework described the procedure generally consists of selecting a panel of experts, asking each to make statements about the future in his area of expertise, and to react to these statements. The reactions may be in terms of probability of occurrence, time of occurrence, desirability, or the like. It is not uncommon to provide the panel of experts with some thought-provoking information at the time they are first asked to make statements about the future. For example, "The first questionnaire presented the respondents with a brief description of current trends in each of twelve areas..."(8) or, "It was deemed prudent to assist panelists in their quest for forecasts with an outline of the topic..."(9) The Delphi technique was used in the present study. The panel of experts was comprised of the chief administrative officers in the English-language teacher education institutions in Canada. In institutions enrolling over 1,000 students, the chief administrative officer was asked to name a panelist for each additional 1,000 students or fraction thereof. (See Table 1).

Part II

TABLE 1

Panelists in Study on Future of Teacher Education

	Contacted	Participated
Universities	30	20
Teachers' colleges	11	7
Number of institutions	41	27
Panelists in universities	43	32
Panelists in colleges	12	8
Number of panelists	55	40

Of the 32 panelists from universities, 15 were deans or
equivalent, 2 were associate deans, 5 were department
heads, and 10 were professors; of those from teachers'
colleges, 7 were presidents or equivalent, and one was
a staff member.

In Part I of the study, each of the 40 panelists who con-
sented to participate was provided with twenty statements
about the future of education and invited to formulate
statements about the future of teacher education. In edited form, these statements became the questionnaire
of Part II of the study, in which panelists were asked to
choose the most probable date of occurrence from given
time intervals. Part III provided data on how the group
as a whole had reacted to some of the statements in
Part II; panelists were asked to reconsider these particular items in light of this information. In Part IV,
panelists were asked to state the most probable date
of occurrence in their own institution. It should be noted
that the original 40 panelists who completed Part I par-
ticipated also in Parts II and III. Thirty-nine panelists
completed Part IV.

STATEMENTS ABOUT THE FUTURE OF EDUCATION

Futurologists point out that the social consequences of technological change present complexities and difficulties of considerable magnitude. It follows that to derive concepts about the future of education is a difficult matter. The future of teacher education, inextricably bound up as it is with the future of education is several stages removed from technological change; for this reason it was decided to provide in Part I a set of statements about the future of education. Dyck's survey (previously mentioned) provided 25; an additional survey of recent literature brought to 58 the number of statements identified. Many of them overlapped; after eliminating the overlap, twenty statements, with references cited, were selected for use. One reason for supplying participants with a selection of statements on the future of education was that these might serve as a model of the type of statement being sought about the future of teacher education.

PANELISTS' STATEMENTS ABOUT THE FUTURE OF TEACHER EDUCATION

Instructions to the panelists were to list, based on their own view of what teacher education would be like in the year 2000, statements about teacher education in the future. Most of the 183 statements received were reasonably terse, in the order of 20 to 50 words. Some were incontestable (e.g., "Teacher education will continue to be concerned with the art of communication.") Others were statements of trend (e.g., "There will be greater emphasis on selection.") Many expressed the same idea in different forms.

The editing process sought to reword trend state-

ments into statements descriptive of a state, to eliminate   overlap, to omit statements with which it was
thought everyone would agree, to sharpen the wording
to increase clarity and avoid ambiguity, and to break
up statements including several ideas, either into
separate statements or into a common stem with mul-
tiple branches. One of the most difficult decisions
was whether to include statements which, while essentially about the future of education, had appended to
them the requirement that teachers would have to be
prepared to meet the changes mentioned. Where it
appeared that the emphasis in the statement was on
the future of education, it was not included. The edited
statements used in Parts II and IV contained 38
statements organized into 28 items, some having a
stem followed by a number of completions.

PANELISTS' DESCRIPTION OF THE FUTURE OF TEACHER EDUCATION

From the following probable dates of occurrence, panelists   were asked to mark the most likely time they
thought the statement would be descriptive of teacher
education: 1971-75, 1975-85, 1985-2000, after 2000,
never. Even though they were deemed to be experts
in teacher education, the precision of forecast did
not appear to warrant a sophisticated mathematical
treatment of the results. For the purposes of this
study, the number or percent of panelists who marked
adjacent time periods and a rounded   estimate
of the most probable date (by five-year intervals) was
used to denote the degree of consensus. For example,
for the statement, "Teacher education will be the
responsibility of universities or university-related
institutions, " 78 percent of the panelists judged the
most probable date of occurrence as 1971-75; and 20

percent, 1975-85. Thus 98 percent of the panelists judged the most probable date in adjacent columns. For this item, the most likely date of occurrence by five-year intervals was determined to be 1975. The first paragraph below includes statements with 90 percent or higher agreement; the second, statements with over 80 percent agreement. For example, in the first item of the second paragraph, 28 percent of the panelists chose the most probable date as 1971-75 and 60 percent as 1975-85. The most likely date of occurrence was determined to be 1980. The succeeding paragraphs present the remaining statements that describe the future of teacher education, with over 70 percent, 60 percent, 50 percent, and 40 percent agreement, respectively. It is obvious that these latter paragraphs represent considerable disagreement or lack of consensus. It should be emphasized that the panelists originated the 38 statements about the future of teacher education listed below; the authors of the study merely edited them into their present form.

VERY HIGH DEGREE OF CONSENSUS (90 % or more of panelist ratings in adjacent-time categories):

1. Teacher education will be the responsibility of universities or university-related institutions (by 1975).
2. Candidates for teacher education, both for admission to preparatory programs and for first certification, will be required to exhibit satisfactory standards of excellence in (1) human relations; ability to relate to young people and old (by 1980); and (2) English usage; appropriate oral and written languages (by 1975).
3. The common learnings required of all teachers will include preparation in the use of the latest educational technology and media (by 1975).

HIGH DEGREE OF CONSENSUS (80-89 percent of panelist ratings in adjacent time categories):

1. Candidates for teacher education, both for admission to preparatory programs and for first certification, will be required to exhibit a satisfactory standard of excellence in mental health; warmth, understanding, poise, absence of hostility, etc. (1980)
2. Teacher education will emphasize the process of learning (observing, classifying, inferring, enquiring, reasoning, remembering) as contrasted with the product information, knowledge, concepts, generalizations by (1975).
3. In the period of 1971-75, teacher education will be just about the same as it was in 1969-70, i.e., there will be change, but it will be gradual.
4. Although there will be a common core of learning for all, each candidate's program will be individually tailored (by 1985).
5. Candidate for teacher education, both for admission to preparatory programs and for first certification will be required to exhibit a satisfactory standard of excellence in speech: articulation, enunciation, modulation, etc. (by 1985).
6. Institutions devoted to the preparation of teachers will disappear (after the year 2000, or never).
7. Teacher education will be producing teachers who are highly specialized both in individualization and in group processes (by 1985).
8. Teacher education will be involved with constant or periodic reevaluation of teachers, who will have to requalify to retain certification (by 1990).
9. Lectures as we now know them will be almost completely displaced by combinations of self-directed study, tutorials, the use of new technology such as computer-dialed instruction, simulation, T.V., microteaching, and the like (by 1985).

CONSIDERABLE CONSENSUS (70-79 percent of panelist ratings in adjacent time categories):

1. The university professor of education will be a
research scholar only (after the year 2,000, or never).
2. Teacher education will be about half common core
for all candidates and about half specific to specialization in terms of function (curriculum materials
developer, diagnostician of learning difficulties, coun-
selor) (by 1985).
3. The common core of learning required of all teachers will include preparation in working as a member and as a leader of a group or team which may be
a mixture of superordinates and subordinates or persons all at one professional level (by 1980).
4. Teacher education will be about half common core
for all candidates and about half specific to specialization in terms of level (nursery to university) (by 1980).
5. Candidates for teaching will have to choose between
two major branches of teacher education: one based on
educational technology (including curriculum development) and the other based on psychology (diagnosis
and prescription of learning) (after the year 2000, or
never).
6. Teacher education will continue throughout the
teachers' career, with frequent use being made of
sabbatical leave arrangements of one or two semes-
ters to be spent in university (by 1985).
7. Teachers and teachers' organizations will share
control of teacher education about equally with teacher education institutions in determining the overall goals of teacher education (by 1980).
8. The majority of professors of education will spend
as much time in the field with children and with teachers as they do in the university (by 1985).

9. Whereas now nearly all teachers are prepared
for teaching at the grades 1-12 (or 13) level up to
half will be prepared for teaching at earlier or
later levels, such as nursery, kindergarten, adult,
and continuing education (by 1985).
10. Teacher education will be centered around an extended internship (by 1985).

SOME CONSENSUS (60-69 percent of panelist ratings
in adjacent time categories):

1. Teacher education will provide limited common-
ality of experience and no established minimum or
maximum time requirement (after the year 2000, or
never).
2. Teacher education will be involved in making education an effective force for reducing social and
other inequalities (by 1980).
3. Teachers and teachers' organizations will share
control of teacher education about equally with teachers education institutions in recruitment and selection of candidates (by 1980).
4. The common core of learning required of all teachers will include an emphasis on ethics, morals,
attitude development, and character formation (by
1990).
5. Certification (or its equivalent) will be specific
to the area of specialization (by 1980).
6. There will be disillusionment with innovation and
change in teacher education (by 1980).
7. General education and subject matter specialization will be relegated to the background in favor of
psychological and sociological studies, studies of
cultural values, guidance techniques, and the like
(after the year 2000, or never).
8. Teachers and teachers' organizations will share

control of teacher education about equally with teacher education institutions (1) in determining the curriculum and procedures used in teacher education institutions (by 1990), and (2) in determining which candidates have successfully completed the program and warrant certification (by 1980).
9. The mass approach to the preparation of teachers will be supplemented by a highly individualized and very expensive sequence of field experiences extending from orientation to teaching to post-program assistance and using extensive human and technetronic resources (by 1990).

LITTLE CONSENSUS(50-59 percent of panelist ratings in adjacent time categories):

1. Teachers will be prepared more intensively as subject specialist (by 1980).
2. Teacher education will be based upon an individual learning contract established directly between the neophyte and a representative board of scholars, professionals, and government representatives, the contract content to be determined by the gap that exists between the student's present capabilities and the minimal standards required for the professional work in which he seeks to specialize (by 1990).
3. Teacher education programs will average six years of university-level preparation before certification (by 1990).
4. Teacher education will be about half common core for all candidates and about half specific to specialization in terms of staff differentiation (teacher, supervisor, administrator) (by 1990).

NO CONSENSUS (Less than 50 percent of panelist ratings in adjacent time categories):

1. The traditional boundaries between discipline and methodology will disappear, i.e., general methods related to the cognitive disciplines will displace specialized methods in specific subjects (by 1980).

A reader reaction may be that these statements deemed by the panelists to be descriptive of teacher education by the dates given offer little that is new or startling. A response to this reaction is that change and improvement in teacher education may be more likely to occur by dissemination, diffusion, and adoption of presently known and used features of teacher education rather than by the invention or discovery of entirely new features. A second response is that if teacher education everywhere had the features described, it would differ considerably from teacher education as it is in fact in many institutions.

It is of considerable interest to compare the statements on which there is a high degree of consensus with those on which there is little. It is also of considerable interest to note that a number of statements originated by their colleagues were rejected (marked as after 2000, or never) by the majority of the panelists. The panelists in this study had firm beliefs about the future of teacher education that were not greatly affected by convergence techniques.

CONVERGENCE

The essence of the Delphi technique as originally conceived was to secure agreement or consensus of experts without the distracting pressures generated from face-to-face or group contact. In the present study, ten statements were resubmitted to the panelists in Part III in an effort to secure convergence; with each one, the percent response from Part II was provided.

In the case of one statement, the comments showed that there were two distinct interpretations. Hence, an additional explanation was provided, and consensus (measured by the response in two adjacent columns) increased from 51 to 81 percent. For three other items, the change was an increase in consensus of 17, 15, and 10 percent, respectively. For two items there was no change; and for one, there was a decrease in consensus as measured. These results hide a change in distribution of response, which frequently occurred. However, this change in response was of considerable magnitude on only four of the ten items; on another four, there was little change.

PANELISTS' DESCRIPTION OF THE FUTURE OF TEACHER EDUCATION IN THEIR OWN INSTITUTIONS

Part IV of the study resubmitted the statements about the future of teacher education to the panelists, with the request that they mark when the statement would be descriptive of teacher education in their own institutions. The time intervals and the method of scoring were the same as for Parts II and III. The authors were interested to determine the relationship between the views of the panelists when responding to teacher education in general and when responding with respect to possible implementation in their own institutions.

Two items were not included in Part IV: one because it was not appropriate for the instructions, and the other because it was the statement previously mentioned as having two distinct interpretations. The

Part II

Spearman rank order correlation between the responses in Part II (as modified by Part III) and Part IV was 0.85. In general, in applying the statements about the future of teacher education to their own institutions, the panelists tended to choose later dates of occurrence. Considerable consistency was evident between what the respondents believe will happen in teacher education in the future and what they believe about the implications and applications in their own colleges and universities. However, the realities of operating in a particular institution seem to have had a conservative effect on opinions about the date of occurrence of specific aspects of teacher education.

CONCLUSION

The authors, although aware of the many limitations of the present study, feel that there is merit in experimenting with the Delphi technique as an alternative to the round-table discussion. In spite of the fact that the respondents in the study are in a variety of teacher education institutions, there is evidence that their professional opinions about the preparation of teachers are more alike than one would anticipate. It seems obvious that the teacher educators and teacher education institutions included in this study are aware of the problems facing education--and hence, teacher education--in the years ahead, and that much careful and creative thought is already being given to the planning and development of programs suited to the needs of the future.

Dr. Clarke is director, Summer Session and Evening Credit Program and Dr. Coutts is dean, Faculty of Education, The University of Alberta, Edmonton, Canada.

Notes and References

1. Burdin, Joel L. , and Lanzillotti, Kaliopee. A
   Reader's Guide to the Models for Preparing Elementary Teachers. Washington, D. C. ; ERIC Clearing-
   house on Teacher Education and American Association of Colleges for Teacher Education, 1969.
2. Clarke, S. C. T. "Designs for Programs of Teacher
   Education. " Research in Teacher Education; A
   Symposium. (Edited by B. O. Smith.) New York:
   Prentice-Hall, 1971.
3. ----. "The Preparation of Instructional Personnel,
   Nursery to Grade 12, to 1999. " Position paper.
   Edmonton, Canada: Alberta Commission on Educational Planning, 1970. (Unpublished)
4. ----. "The Story of Elementary Teacher Education
   Models. " The Journal of Teacher Education 20:
   283-93; Fall, 1969.
5. Coutts, H. T. "Preparing the Teachers We Need. "
   Edmonton, Canada: University of Alberta, 1970.
   (Unpublished)
6. Cyphert, Frederick R. , and Gant, Walter L. "The
   Delphi Technique: A Case Study. " Phi Delta Kappan
   52: 272-73; January, 1971.
7. ----. "The Delphi Technique: A Tool for Collecting
   Opinions in Teacher Education. " The Journal of
   Teacher Education 21:417-25; Fall, 1970.
8. de Brigard, Paul, and Helmer, Olaf. Some Potential
   Societal Development, 1970-2000. Middletown,
   Conn. ; Institute for the Future, 1970.
9. Dyck, Harold J. "Alberta's Future: Social Life, 1970-
   2005. " An Interim Report on the Alberta Delphi Interaction Studies. " Edmonton, Canada: Westrede Institute,
   1970.

Notes and References (cont'd)

10. Dyck, Harold J., and others. "An Outline of the Future: Some Facts, Forecasts, and Fantasies." Edmonton, Canada: Human Resources Research Council, 1970.

11. Educational Policy Research Center. "Aims and Functions of the Educational Policy Research Center." Menlo Park, Calif.: Stanford Research Institute, n. d.

12. Europe 2000. Fondation Europeenne de la Culture. Volumes 1 to 5. Fifth edition. Amsterdam: Jan Vangoyenkade, 1970.

13. Helmer, Olaf, and Rescher, Nicholas. "On the Epistemology of the Inexact Sciences." Management Science 6; 1959.

14. Klatt, Judith, and Le Baron, Walt. A Short Summary of Ten Model Teacher Education Programs. USOE Report Washington, D. C.: Government Printing Office, 1969.

15. Le Baron, Walt. Analytical Summaries of Specifications for Model Teacher Education Programs USOE Report. Falls Church, Va.: Systems Development Corporation, 1969.

16. ----Techniques for Developing an Elementary Teacher Education Model: A Short Review of Models, Systems, Analysis and Learning Systems, USOE Report. Falls Church, Va.: Systems Development Corporation, 1969.

17. Michigan State University. Feasibility Study: Behavioral Science Teacher Education Program. USOE Report. Lansing, Mich.: the University, 1970

18. Morphet, Edgar, L., and Jesser, David L., editors. Preparing Educators To Meet Emerging Needs. New York: Citation Press, 1969.

Notes and References (cont'd)

19. Schalock, H. Del; Kersh, Bert Y. ; and Horyna,
    Larry L. A Plan for Managing the Development,
    Implementation and Operation of a Model Elemen-
    tary Teacher Education Program, USOE Report.
    Washington, D. C. ; Government Printing Office
    1969.
20. Sowards, J. W. A Model for the Preparation of
    Elementary School Teachers. USOE Report.
    Washington, D. C.; Government Printing Office,
    1968.
21. Weaver, W. Timothy. "The Delphi Forecasting
    Method. " Phi Delta Kappan, 52:267-71; January
    1971.
22. Weber, Wilford A. A Study of the Feasibility
    of the Refined Syracuse University Specifications
    for a Comprehensive Undergraduate and Inservice
    Teacher Education Program for Elementary
    Teachers. USOE Report. Washington, D. C. ;
    Government Printing Office, 1969.
23. Ziegler, Warren L. "Some Notes on How Educa-
    tional Planning in the United States looks at the
    Future. " Notes on the Future of Education 1;
    November-December 1969.

Part III

CONCEPTUAL VIEWS

OF THE FUTURE

For I dipt into the future,
far as human eye could see,
Saw the Vision of the world,
and all the wonder that would be;
Saw the heavens fill with commerce,
argosies of magic sails,
Pilots of the purple twilight,
dropping down with costly bales . . .
Till the war drum throbbed no longer
and the battle flags were furled
In the Parliament of Man,
the Federation of the world.

LORD TENNYSON

"Locksley Hall"

Herman Cohn in Retrospect:
A Parable for Futurists

Harrison Brown

SHORTLY AFTER THE TURN OF THE CENTURY,
A NOW FORGOTTON FUTURIST NAMED HERMAN
COHN FORESAW THE PROBLEMS THAT WOULD BE
CREATED BY AUTOMOBILES AND MECHANIZATION
OF AGRICULTURE. COHN WAS HORRIFIED BY HIS
OWN FORECASTS, BUT HE REMAINED OPTIMISTIC.
"ONCE OUR POLITICAL LEADERS ARE TOLD THIS
STORY," HE SAID CONFIDENTLY, "THEY WILL
TAKE ACTIONS WHICH ARE NECESSARY TO BRING
ABOUT A MORE PALATABLE FUTURE."

It has often been said that we cannot understand the
future without first understanding the past. And so,
I would like to start by relating an obscure tale from
American history.

The writings of one Herman Cohn, an early futurist,
are not very well known, even to the specialist. Herman was science consultant to William Jennings Bryan
during his 1908 campaign, and he was confident that
one day he would be chairman of the President's
Science Advisory Committee. Cohn had been hired by
Bryan because of a misunderstanding which might well
have resulted from poor hearing. When asked by
Bryan whether Herman Cohn was a Fundamentalist,
Cohn had replied, "Yes, I am fundamental." Bryan
then said: "Young man, you are hired."

Reprinted from the Fall, 1971, issue of Education Horizon
with the permission of the author and Pi Lambda Theta.

Part III

Following Bryan's final defeat, Herman Cohn drift-
ed. For some time he headed a small not-for-prof-
it corporation called Prediction, Inc., but his
clients tended to be antagonized by his predictions.
When he forecast the demise of the bustle, his one
remaining client withdrew and the business failed.
Eventually Herman fell into obscurity as Professor
of Social Physics at Yale. He died a thin, malnour-
ished, broken man.

Recently, when an old home in New Haven was torn
down to make room for a parking lot, a bundle of
Cohn's unpublished manuscripts was discovered.
I have had the good fortune of examining some of
these writings and I now understand why Herman
was not very popular. For one thing, he was what
we today would call a "Prophet of Doom." For another, unlike most futurists, he was supremely confident of his conclusions.

I will skip over a rather bulky essay written in 1908
entitled On Nitroglycerine War, which was obviously
written to impress William Jennings Bryan with the
importance of maintaining a strong defense establishment. I will also pass over other essays such as The
Decline and Fall of the British and French Empires,
The Coming Russian Superstate and Will Railroads
Become Obsolete? None of these, incidentally, were
accepted for publication. Instead, I would like to draw
your attention to yet another rejected manuscript entitled The Social and Political Consequences of the Internal Combustion Engine, written in 1916, just 55 years
ago.

In this essay, Herman Cohn agreed with his fellow
futurists of the day that the automobile was here to

stay and that machines powered by gasoline engines
would one day do virtually all of the work on the farms.
But whereas other futurists pointed only to the joyous
aspects of this new development, Herman Cohn alone
forecast trouble. "I agree, " he said, "that it would
be pleasant to walk on streets free of animal waste
products. But can we be sure that the waste products
of the automobile will be an improvement?"

Cohn predicted that the attraction of the human being
to the automobile would be irresistible. He discusses
several aspects of human sensuousness and suggests
that the automobile will eventually become what he
calls a "societal position indicator, " which I gather
is what we today refer to as a "status symbol. " He
predicted that people would eventually reach the point
where they would be willing to do virtually anything
to acquire one. "So intense will their desires become,"
he suggests, "they will even be willing to forego bearing children, if by so doing they might hasten the day
when one of these machines will be theirs alone. " He
concludes that we will eventually reach the point where
every adult in the nation will own an automobile.

With respect to the farm, Cohn points out that the
attraction of the farmer to the tractor is equally
irresistible, although in this case the attraction stems
from strictly economic considerations rather than
for reasons involving sensuousness or societal position indicators. He concludes that farm labor will
eventually disappear from the earth scene.

Assuming the persistence of these two basic forces--
the attraction between human and automobile and that
between farmer and tractor--Herman Cohn then pro-
ceeds to develop what he calls "the sequence of events

which I would be most likely to bet money on. " In
this sequence, which today we call a scenario(There
were no motion pictures at that time.), he describes
the introduction of the automobile to the city, the
struggle between automobile and horse, followed by
the demise of the latter, the frantic attempts to a-
dapt the city so as better to accommodate the automobile, the increasing congestion, the emergence
of the parking lot, the freeway and the service sta-
tion with restrooms.

BLACK GHETTOES FORESEEN

Cohn then turns his attention to the rural areas and
asks, '"What will happen to the labor force when the
machines take over the farms ? " He predicted that
the displaced farm laborers would flock to the cities
and he pointed out that being poor, they could not just
settle anywhere. Using the analogy of the 19th century
wave of immigrants from Europe to the United States,
he suggested that large ghetto areas would emerge
and the skin complexion of the residents would be predominantly black. He suggested further that the newly
found mobility of the middle class would result in
massive migration from the cities to the country-side
where "they can live in comfortable homes, isolated
from the depressing sights and sounds of poverty, ignorance, and violence. "

Herman Cohn predicted the rise and fall of effective
public transportation systems and concluded, "Cities
will become mixtures of office buildings, factories,
parking areas, and highways, all imbedded in extensive black slums, which in turn will be surrounded at
a safe distance by comfortable white residential areas. "
He describes the sensitivity to disruption of a complex

organism such as a city and concludes that the major
cities in the United States are destined to cease func-
tioning as the result of violence and disruption or as
the result of prolonged disintegration or more likely
both. "New York City, " Cohn wrote, "will grow to become a metropolis of more than ten million persons
and will spread over three states. Manhattan Island
will become a vast slum unfit for human habitation.
Eventually the congestion, the filth and decay will
combine with instability with respect to disruption,
and the entire organism will cease to function. "

Cohn, who was obviously horrified by his own forecast, quickly pointed out that his conclusions were
based simply upon an extrapolation of then-current
trends. "Once our political leaders are told this
story, " he said confidently, "they will take the actions which are necessary to bring about a more
palatable future. " He clearly viewed the science and
art of forecasting as a mechanismfor bringing existing and potential societal problems to the attention
of lawmakers.

The final paragraph of this essay is particularly re-
vealing:

"Our political leaders at the city, county, state and
national levels are intelligent and practical persons
who know how to get things done. Thus far this work
has been confined almost entirely to the solution of
critical current problems. It seems clear that they
must now begin to devote time and energy to the solution of problems before they actually become problems. I am confident that once our leaders read
these forecasts, they will take actions which are designed to forestall the predicted end result. "

This was Herman Cohn's final essay. Records indicate that he talked with many city councilmen, state legislators, and congressmen. The same records indicate that he became increasingly frustrated and depressed. In a letter written to one of his few friends he said, 'They are always suspicious and on guard when I talk about possible happenings 50 or even 25 years from now. They look at me with some mild, even tolerant, amusement and smile as though to say, "You are interrupting my concentration on critical immediate problems.' They take the attitude that the future is for those who live in the future to handle. "

Herman Cohn died shortly after he wrote those words.

Harrison Brown (B.S., University of California; Ph.D., Johns Hopkins University) is professor of geochemistry and professor of science and government at California Institute of Technology.

Beyond Tomorrow—What?

Harvey Wheeler

.... WE HAVE THE CAPABILITY OF REDESIGNING,
REDEVELOPING, AND REVITALIZING DEMOCRACY
AND MAKING IT APPLICABLE IN A PARTICIPATIONAL
SENSE TO ALL OF OUR CITIZENS FOR THE FIRST
TIME IN HISTORY.

I'm going to talk about the future, the future in general,
and then about revolution, which seems to be part of
the future. Under revolution, I'll first say what I think
revolution is and then discuss its two primary components, the scientific revolution and the cultural revolution; we can't have a meeting anywhere in the United
States today without talking about the cultural revolu-
tion--the Greening of America. In conclusion, I'll
discuss the prospects for revolution.

First, a word about one of the most popular indoor
symposium exercises of our time--the subject that
is called Futurology, which is ostensibly the thing I've
been asked to talk about here. Futurology is quite popular today. Most universities now have one or more
courses solely devoted to it. It is a strange thing to
live in times in which one of the social sciences is
Futurology. There was a time when the social sciences
dealt with political theory, economics, and things like
that.

What kind of validity can you expect when you try to talk

Reprinted from the Fall, 1971, issue Educational Horizons,
with the permission of the author and Pi Lambda Theta.

about things that lie beyond the horizon of time?
Most people who do this, Herman Kahn is an example,
deal in what we call linear projections. They look at
a few things that are going on now, they estimate rates
of increase or decrease over the past few years, then
they assume these trends will continue into the future,
and, on this basis, they construct a picture of what the
future will be like in 30 years or so. This is what we
call a linear projection. Linear projections are satisfactory for some purposes, such as estimating world
steel capacity ten years hence, but for anything in
which there may be a surprise, a major innovation,
such projections are of limited value. Suppose that
next year someone invents a structural material to
supplant steel. Of what use is the ten-year linear projection made the year before? For most problems
linear projections are even less reliable than this. But
we still make them because we don't know how to make
non-linear projections.

Linear projections are even more hazardous when we
try to apply them to social institutions. Most of us can
recall projections made in our own businesses concerning sales or prices or profits that have turned
out to be wrong. Some of you may have seen the Satur-
day Review article on Jean-Francois Revel's new
book, Neither Marx nor Jesus. This is a brilliant
book, but it was tripped up by a linear projection.
Revel finished his book in 1969, while visiting the
Center for the Study of Democratic Institutions. Like
many others, he assumed the "Woodstock Nation"
was here to stay, and based part of his book upon that
assumption. A year later, just in time for the reviewers
to note it, Fillmore East and West had both closed and
the Woodstock Nation had given away to the "Summer
of '42. "

There is another projection that is popular in educational circles today--a report by Alan Cartter. Many of you know about this because it predicts what the market for higher education is going to be in a few years. Alan Cartter is a very good economist and a very good linear projector. He has observed current population trends and the income trend and so he predicts a massive depression in higher education.

The world we're getting into now is going to last for another generation and, according to demographic projections, this looks like a pretty sensible thing to say. And I know all my colleagues are scared to death. Today there is a buyers' market in intellectuals, a situation that is pleasing only to buyers. But there are other factors to consider. For example, we've had a decade of dropouts in higher education; today, however, educators are talking about dropins. If you drop out, you've got to drop in to something. But life experience experimentation is not very nourishing as a steady diet. Now what yesterday's dropouts want is to understand the world. They are beginning to re-enroll, seeking a more fundamental understanding of the World. They may not want degrees, but I do believe the market for higher education is going to expand by attracting the very students who formerly dropped out. This will change course offerings. It will also change the age mix in our classrooms. We shall see a new cross-generational education.

Consider also the advent of the four-day week. What will a four-day week mean? Maybe one thing it will mean will be the advent of the three-day university. So my guess is that Cartter is absolutely wrong.

Part III

Having said this, I am going to make a projection,
but I shall do so on what seems to be a sound historical ground. These are, mind you, revolutionary
times and the evidence of this is pretty good. We
are living today in a profoundly revolutionary period.
There are few times in previous history that have
been as earth-shaking in their revolutionary potential.
One of these was in Greece in the fifth century, B. C.
Plato and Aristotle were writing at that time and both
of them, as well as most of the other intellectuals
around them, knew very well that the end of the polis
was at hand. That was their whole story. Plato and
Aristotle both pondered the implications of this prospect. They lived in a time of revolution and upheaval,
the watershed between hellenic and hellenistic times.
Those brilliant men were very accurate in perceiving
the causes of their revolutionary turmoil.

Another very brilliant futurologist who lived in revolutionary times was St. Augustine. A host of people
around his time also saw the end of the Roman Em-
pire, but he was most perceptive and he found out why
it was breaking up and what was coming after. In fact,
the theology he worked out in rudimentary form at
that time became the foundation for Christian theology during the next two thousand years. St. Augustine
was an extremely brilliant futurologist.

The next futurologist was Francis Bacon, who lived
at the birth of the Industrial Revolution. Bacon made
very profound projections. Many of the people of his
time understood what was going on: what was dying,
what was being born, and what the implications of
this were. These were futurologists of great genius
who based their assessments upon their analysis of
trends observable in revolutionary times.

So my contention is that if one takes a sufficiently
broad scope and if one happens to live in revolutionary times, there is some chance of making fairly
reliable projections about the future. So let us try
our hand at it.

I want to say briefly what I think our own revolutionary period is like. It is one that can be talked
about in terms of Charles Dickens' opening phrase
in A Tale of Two Cities: " It was the best of times,
it was the worst of times, " and then he went on to
tell the tale of two cities. One was revolutionary,
Paris: and the other was the counter-revolutionary,
London. This seems to me to provide a very useful
and accurate clue to the nature of a revolutionary
period. It is one in which the society has split in
two. It has become, in effect, two cities. It becomes
something like today's op art; the entire society
takes on the aspects of an optical illusion. You look
at it one day and the Establishment is securely in
the saddle. Everything is fine and it's the best of
all worlds. You look at the society five minutes
later--or the next day--and you will see the same things,
but they all seem to be the opposite of what they had
been just before. You see its difficulties--the turmoil,
the violence, the counter movements; you see what is
failing. Everything seems to be falling down. You see
the second city--the underground city--and this now
dominates your vision. Every institution you look at
is in crisis--schools, family, everything. And yet
both views are right and both are contained within
one society. That is why I like this notion of its being
two cities comprised in one. The fact that this con-
tainer, this society, is dualistic, a dual city, is to
me the essence of revolution. Revolution is the dialectic expression of the conflict between these two
social systems.

Part III

Another characteristic of a revolutionary period like
our own is that it has a special kind of crisis. Now
crisis is something we always have in history in
every society. That is one of the reasons we have
social institutions such as courts, a family system,
an economic system, and so on. One of the things
the institutions do is resolve crises. They each have
their own particular crises. There are crises in the
schools and we have the Parent-Teacher Association,
the school boards and many other associations to
resolve them.

Normally, these institutions and their crisis-resolving
procedures have done very well. When students got
out of hand, for example, there would be a meeting of
parents and teachers, some kind of reform would
follow, new people would be appointed to a committee;
they protest about being co-opted, and somebody tries
to blow up the committee. Wherever one looks today,
there are such crises. They are met by attempts to
apply the traditional procedures that have been able to
resolve crises in the past, and the result of the application of traditional procedures is that things are worse
afterwards than they were before. The use of the very
procedures that were developed to resolve crises
results instead in their aggravation.

In the political order as a whole, the same kind of
thing happens. This produces a revolutionary situation.
A situation with a high potential for revolution is one
in which this special kind of crisis occurs frequently:
a crisis in which the attempt to apply traditional procedures that are supposed to resolve it results in the
aggravation rather than the amelioration of the crisis,
and that aggravation, in making things worse, serves
the function of high-lighting the contradictions between
the two cities. Today it seems that we're all in this
kind of a crisis situation.

Revolution does not always mean violence in the
streets. That was not the nature of the revolution
described by Plato and Aristotle, or that of St.
Augustine or even of the Industrial Revolution, although all of them had a great deal of violence.
But evolutionary times, too, have violence. Violence as such is not what we mean by revolution.
Rather, we refer to the deeper forces of institutional disruption that are asserting themselves
today. These are the forces we wish to make the
bases for our projections.

Today's revolutionary situation has the two chief
components I mentioned earlier. The first of them
is the scientific revolution and the second is the
cultural revolution. It is not necessary to give extensive consideration to the cultural revolution
since this has been widely discussed. But what do
we mean by the scientific revolution?

Today we are entering what is increasingly called
the post-industrial era. We've all seen this phrase;
it is referred to every other week in the Sunday sup-
plements. But what do people mean when they speak
of the post-industrial world? Well, obviously it
refers in some sense to the end of the industrial
world. That much is obvious. But more than this,
it means the advent of the scientific revolution. This
is symbolized in the difference between an enerygy
source like the TVA and thermonuclear power. The
earlier one was produced by technological extensions
of familiar engineering techniques. It applied the industrial methods we've been familiar with for a couple
of hundred years. The new one rested upon entirely
novel and abstruse scientific theories. This meant
theoreticians were the chief--what would you call
them--entrepreneurs? That isn't strictly true be-

cause, of course, they were not money makers in
any direct sense. They were highly paid, but the
main thing is that they were the chief architects of
the energy source.

There are two characteristics we see when we compare an earlier industrial enterprise like building
a dam with later, more scientific enterprises like
thermonuclear energy. We see that the relationship
between theory and practice is reversed. In the old
days, technology, in an overt sense, was the foundation; and theory, if it was around at all, was merely
to embellish the practical know-how that provided
the foundation of industry. Now, theory is the foundation and technology is the means of realizing what has
been developed in theory. Related to that reversal is
the reversal in the positions of the practitioner and
the theoretician. Previously, we used to say that the
practitioner, the practical man of affairs, was on
top and the theoretician was, as the British say about
the civil servant, on top. He was a handmaiden, a
servant. Now that relationship is reversed. Increasingly the theoretician is the person who is on top and
the practical man of affairs has a somewhat lower
position in the scale of things. So this is the essence
of what we mean by the scientific revolution.

As we move into the post-industrial world, a scientific
innovation will be the determining thing. This is the
third aspect. In the industrial world we saw the flow
of capital as being the dominant force. If one could
control the flow of capital, it was possible to control
the society. That is what Karl Marx said and most
people believed it. Marx wrote of the world of the
capitalist and the Industrial Revolution. We didn't
agree with all the conclusions Marx came to, but

his analysis has been incorporated into our standard
history of the nature of the flow of capital and its
importance. What about the post-industrial world?
There we are talking about the flow of innovation
and invention in the scientific sense. To carry out the
analogy, the control of the flow of innovation would
be the dominating feature of the world of the scientific revolution.

Consider the nature of innovations. We used to call
them inventions. We don't call them inventions any
more--not very often anyway, because the term
"invention" calls up the idea of Henry Ford, Thomas
Alva Edison, Alexander Graham Bell, and so on.

In this country after the Civil War, almost every
year saw the appearance of a new invention. Sewing
machines, reapers, telephones, phonographs, and
so on--a wild proliferation of inventions for about
50 to 75 years right up to World War II. These were
inventions that were all extensions of human capacities. They extended the power of a woman to
make a dress. The human voice could be carried
further because of the telephone. Tools extended
the capacity of the hand, and so on.

What kinds of innovations have occurred since World
War II? The curious thing is that this has been a
sterile time. We've had two important innovations:
thermonuclear power, produced by World War II,
and the computer, combining energy and thought.
Now what kinds of innovations are these? They are
not like the older inventions that enhanced man's
individual capacities. These are Promethean: we
rob energy from the sun, thought from the brain.
This is an entirely new world. Neither of these

innovations has yet found a mass market potential--
not like any one of the great nineteenth century or
early twentieth century inventions. But if and when
they do, it will be fantastic. The changes brought
by automobiles and freeways will be nothing compared
to those to   accompany the home computer hooked
up to multi-media consoles. We'll come back to
this later, but the point here is that the nature of
innovation has changed entirely. It is not merely
the extension of individual human capacities; these
now are systemic inventions. Beyond energy and
thought there is life. The biological revolution is
rushing upon us with its promise of expanded lon-
gevity, synthetic life forms, and genetic engineering.
But consider thought, energy, life. These are the
kinds of inventions we are getting now; and no matter how one looks at revolution, this is revolution--
the scientific revolution!

If we are to sit down here, lock the doors, and form
a conspiracy to get control of society, we would aim
at getting control of the forces at work in this scientific revolution; for example, we would try to get
control of the total national budget for scientific
research. This would allow us to decide what sciences and technologies would be fostered and applied,
whether to seek for healthier and longer lives
through biology or more spectacular advances in
space explorations. If we could get control of the
total national budget, both public funds and those
spent privately in corporations and foundations on
science, that mere achievement would give us the
ability to decide which way the culture would develop
10 to 15 years from now. Because if you decide
you're going to have a life support system for human
beings here on earth in biology or a life support system

for people traveling through space, the space program (both are massive investments), whichever
way you go will have a tremendous influence on the
nature of the culture when that investment bears
fruit. The ability to control science could make the
difference between a space-born culture or a health-
ful culture. Whoever made the decision would, in
effect, be the legislature: a new kind of legislature.
In fact, such science policy issues are the kinds of
problems that are arising ever more frequently today. This is the next topic.

Our present legislature, meaning Congress with its
two chambers, is only one way of legislating. It
was a way that was invented, or developed, in the
eighteenth century. It didn't come out of the Garden
of Eden with Adam and Eve. It was fresh and bright
and shiny and radical--revolutionary in the eighteenth century. It was revolutionary because it was
very well adapted to the problems of the industrial
age, the one we're leaving. Now we have a new
revolution, the scientific revolution. New kinds of
problems and decision-making processes are needed
for those new problems which simply are not resolv-
able through the traditional institutions. Here is another form of the crisis described earlier.

Let me give you an example. One of the things we
will soon be able to do out of the biological revolution is to determine the sex of children. The moment
we find that there is a pregnancy we can go to our
family molecular biologist and have a treatment and
determine whether the baby is going to be a boy or
girl. Everybody will be able to do this. All right,
what will we do when everybody is able to choose
whether they will have boys or girls? Let people de-

cide according to their whims? If we do this, what
are they going to decide? Suppose a large majority
of the people decide in favor of one sex or the other.
What would be the effect on society if it were com-
posed predominantly of one sex? Or if it alternated
from one sex to the other in different generations?
If we leave people to decide this matter individually
we may have a very, very strange-looking population. Moreover, it would cause grave problems we
don't now know how to handle. What would we do with
a population like that? If we do leave people to decide
individually what they want and decide to take the
social consequences, that is a form of public policy,
isn't it? We say, in effect, we'll take our chances
with what people will decide, regardless of what it
is. That's our public policy. The point is that we
cannot escape having a public policy on this issue.
It's here, and if we say we're not going to do anything formally about it--that's a public policy. But
most people would probably think that 75 percent of
either sex would be too much. The proportion ought
to be less than that. But how would we resolve the
question of how much less? What is the guideline?
What is the right balance of the sexes for the population? How would we decide? Who knows the answer?
It is a very complicated question that involves a lot
of scientific information. Normally our legislatures
decide such questions. But think what would happen
if we threw this kind of question to the Congress in
Washington as it functions today? How would Congress
deal with this question? Not very well. Yet this is
one of the simplest of the new science-related questions that will face us.

Our next concern is the computer. No one doubts
that the computer will have a revolutionizing effect

on our society, especially when it achieves widespread consumer application. So far, what we've
done with the computer is very simple. We just
pull out the human beings from telephone switch-
boards and put computers in their places. The
system still operates except that we've got computers there instead of people. A similar thing
happened when the internal combustion engine
was first invented. We took buggies and merely
removed the horses and installed engines where
the horses had been. It took a long, long time to
get the VW and the Ferrari, that is, to discover
and apply the internal logic of the gasoline engine.
The same thing is happening now with the computer.
We're just coming to the point where its own internal logic, its own rationality, is beginning to
assert itself. The problem is not merely to substitute computers for people the way engines were
substituted for horses; the rationale of the computer system must be developed and applied.

Let us recount a few of the things that are taking
place. But first a caveat. We are not going to get
magic out of computers. They don't do either of
the two things that we want them to: they don't
tell us what is right and they don't make decisions.
But we will be able to do many things that could
not be done before and we will be able to do them
quite rapidly. To do this, however, we must tell
the computer what is right and what is wrong. We
must put our values into it in the beginning. That
is one of the nicest things about the computer. It
forces us to think about what we believe in. We
can hide this from ourselves for a long time, but
when we face a computer, we have to decide what
we want. The computer forces us to think.

Secondly, the computer produces alternatives. It
gives us probabilities. It stands there and chatters
them out and makes us decide. These qualifications
are very important but still the computer can take
a sophisticated computer and put our values in it
with regard to a city, a city of, say, 200,000 people.
We can define the different things we are interested
in: the educational system, the tax rate, the green-
ery in and around the city, and so on. The computer
displays I have seen can deal with about six different variables of this kind. We can then plot where
the buildings are, where the railroads are, where
the streams are, where the forests are, and
where the disease rate is highest. Then we can have
the computer present a map of the city that is just
like other maps that we've seen before: cultural maps
of cities, land use maps, economic maps, disease
maps, and so on. We can superimpose all six of
these on each other and see the whole demographic,
cultural, educational, economic, and health picture
of the city at once. Then the computer can answer
a lot of questions for us. Suppose we want to put a
new superhighway in this city and we draw a route
on the map; the computer can tell us what will happen to all of our six factors as a result of this particular highway route. This means we can plan our
city developments with much more wisdom then before. We can use several criteria for a highway;one
that is speedy, one that goes through the center of
town, one that goes around the town, one that passes
pleasant things to see, or one that takes us through
slums. Then we can compare each alternative with
the others on the basis of the effect of each upon
the six original factors.

At the present time, we make such decisions in the

dark. Soon we may be able to make computer-assisted displays, like that just described, widely available to citizens. This would have an extremely powerful effect on politics and on decision-making. It
would allow ordinary citizens to understand extremely complex problems and to participate in decisions
about them. We can think of this capacity extended
in many ways. We can think of two people working
a computer together--let's say a Black Power advocate from the ghetto and a banker from some suburb. They want the highway put in different places
because of their different interests. Each can be
given a weighted vote in accordance with the distribution of community power. This gives us a
power confrontation. In such a way we can foresee
something about the likely outcome of a political
power struggle. This means that the computer can
help us visualize in advance the range of compro-
mises open to us. The process of conflict resolution
can be explored well in advance of an actual show-
down.

With another computer program we can depict the
architecture, the actual buildings, of a city in three
dimensions. We can see them on the screen. Then
we can drive through the city with the computer. We
can see what would happen to various buildings if
we put a street in one place rather than in another.
Whereas the first program dealt with the institutions
of a city, this one deals with its physical content.

Next we can visualize a time not too far distant when
computer graphic display terminals will be available
for installation in individual homes. These will be
multimedia installations that can be hooked up to a
vast number of computer-assisted instruction pro-

Part III

grams. These are controversial and deservedly so. But my own view is that the problem is with the software, not with the hardware. Most of the instruction programs have simply been bad programs, and on the basis of bad programs we have concluded that there is something wrong with computer-assisted instruction. I think this will be remedied through a more careful application of operant conditioning techniques. When this occurs, a new vista in adult education will open out before us. For the first time we shall be able to reach the functional illiterate. This will be the hard core problem of the scientific revolution, and the future of democracy depends upon how well we solve it. Some of the studies that have been done indicate that, with good operant conditioning programs, computer-assisted instruction in multimedia installations can in theory begin with an adult, hard core, functional illiterate and, within about a ten-year period, maybe much shorter, give him a college level education.

The thing that is challenging here is that if anything like this possibility exists, it means we have the capability of redesigning, redeveloping, and revitalizing democracy and making it applicable in a participational sense to all of our citizens for the first time in history. Even the extremely complex issues of the scientific revolution described earlier can be analyzed and made understandable and, through increased educational efforts along these lines, be so widely distributed throughout society that the dreams we had for participational democracy in the nineteenth century may acquire a new lease on life.

This is the great promise of the scientific revolution. However, it is going to be hard for us to realize because we are now in a race between Utopia and catastrophe. I've been talking about the Utopian aspects, but we all know from Paul Ehrlich and others who have studied problems relating to pollution and the ecological crisis that there is not much time left. Now I shall not go into the arguments concerning the ecological crisis. In my opinion the situation is grave. My conclusion is that many of the potentials I've been talking about are going to be realized, but they're going to be realized only if we sacrifice many of the quantitative aspects that we've associated in the past with out industrial civilization: the gadgetry, the affluence, the luxuries. These, it seems to me, will have to go--because there are not enough resources in the world to maintain them.

This is a world of a little over three billion people. Six percent of them are Americans. Those Americans use something like 35 percent of the world's critical resources. The rate of population growth is such that the world will contain seven billion by the year 2000. The American proportion is going to drop from six percent to something like five percent or four-and-a-half percent because the expansion of population will occur primarily in the non-American areas of the world. The non-American areas of the world want the good things of life and what they call the good things of life are the things that we have. Just figure it out. Six percent of the people now are using 35 percent of the world's resources and the other 94 percent want the same things as the favored six percent. There simply are not enough resources. The people of the world cannot become Americanized. In fact, America is probably going to have to become dis-Americanized.

Part III

We are living now at the end of a very, very glorious
regime, something like the Ancien regime in 1789 in
France. The old order in France was great--for the
elite, for the aristocracy. Yes, everything was great
for them while it lasted, but it surely was different
afterwards. By the same token, we are now at the end
of the road for the affluent industrial society. There
is more luxury now, and there are more good things
for more people than ever will be available again.
From the standpoint of gadgetry, it is probably down-
hill all the way from here on out through time.

Of course, Americans will have better health. They
will live more rational and more decent lives. They
will buy refrigerators to last for 10 to 15 years instead of one and half or two. They will buy pop-up
toasters that really pop up and really last. Well, these
things are going to be quite great. We're going to have
a better quality of life. That is the true meaning of
the cultural revolution. It means that political and
cultural values are going to change both in this country and throughout the world as the Industrial Revolution comes to an end. It means the development of an
ethic that values the quality of life rather than the
quantity of life.

We have all heard about the zero population growth
movement. Soon we'll be talking about negative population growth movement. We'll be saying, "Don't
have any children. Instead, go out and adopt them. "
Next, there will be the zero economic growth movement. In the past, we have experienced a four percent or five percent a year growth in Gross National
Product. We cannot stand this any longer. The world
as a whole is not able to go on growing this way.
There are just not enought resources to support it.

One of the big things coming is the energy crisis.
People talk about the blue whales dying. Listen,
the extinction of the blue whale is a sad thing but
the energy crisis is something that could strike us
all. The new clean energy physicist say we may
get fusion power. Newspapers write that it can
solve all our problems. Physicists, high energy
physicists, say that it is at least 30 years away.
Yet the rate of energy consumption is doubling
every 14 years and we don't have enough energy
right now. The race that we're in is between eco-
cide, the murder of the environment, and the promise of a Utopian future.

There are many factors in favor of the Utopian
forces, but it is doubtful that they can occur unless
there is a coalescence of the two revolutions we
have described earlier: the bringing together of the
cultural and the scientific revolutions! Until this
liaison is made, it doesn't seem to me that the
forces driving us toward catastrophe can be staved
off. But if we can make this liaison, then the odds
are very good that we will be able to enjoy a much
more wholesome and much more beautiful and much
higher quality future than men have known any time
in the past.

Harvey Wheeler (A. B. , M. A. , Indiana University;
Ph. D. ,Harvard University) is a senior fellow at
the Center for the Study of Democratic Institutions
in Santa Barbara, California. He came to the Center
in 1960 from Washington and Lee University in Lex-
ington, Virginia, where he was a professor of political science. After having served in military government in the European theater during World War II,
he taught political science at Harvard University and
at Johns Hopkins University before going to Washington and Lee.

Schools and Communities: A Look Forward

Thomas F. Green

THE SIGNIFICANT QUESTION IS "DARE THE SOCIAL ORDER BUILD A NEW SYSTEM OF SCHOOLS?"

The following remarks are organized around two concerns. The first is topical; the second is methodological. The topical matter is that durable problem of the relationships between schools and their communities. However, I shall examine this topic from a perspective on the future. Thus, the methodological difficulties are those implicit in any attempt to think about the fairly remote future. Either of these concerns, taken individually, is difficult enough to warrant extended treatment. Taken in combination, they produce overwhelming potentialities for misunderstanding. It may therefore be useful to consider what these reflections are not concerned with and what kinds of claims are not intended.

In the first place, I do not wish to concentrate upon the immediate future. There are so many imponderables in the details of the next five years that I would not venture to anticipate the story. Even a casual glance over the past eighteen months should demonstrate how foolhardy it would be to attempt a detailed picture of the next five years. But if we focus upon a

more remote period, then the singularities of events
that might intrude in the near future becomes less
important, and we can more easily ask questions a-
bout the basic plot rather than about specific events.
I intend, therefore, to fix attention upon a period
ten to twenty years ahead. Though it may be beyond
our reach to predict the precise nature of school
and community relations in the 1980's, nonetheless
it is possible to judge what we can reasonably expect to happen. And among the different states of
affairs we might imagine, it will be more reasonable to expect some than to expect others. For example, it is more   reasonable to assert that the
future holds events which nobody expects than it is
to believe in a world where no such events occur.
A future which contains no surprises is more surprising than one which does. If an expected set of
events or state of affairs does not occur, still it may
be true that it was more reasonable to have expected
it than to have expected something else perhaps even
more reasonable than to have expected what in fact
did occur.[1]

Man's desire to know the future may be among his
most basic characteristics. The Church Fathers
regarded it as evidence of man's sinful nature, and
the ancient Hebrews had a great deal to say about
the human disposition to want to live in knowledge
of the future rather than in faith. It is not likely
that men shall outlive the desire to know the future.
But unless we believe that human affairs are governed entirely by fate, then the capacity to predict
could only serve the human purpose of making those
predictions false. That is to say, unless Moira pre-
vails, the only purpose in wanting to know the future
would be to take such actions and to make such

choices now so that the future would be different.
It is interesting to note how fundamental is the human
demand to know the future. It is even more interesting to note, however, that our purpose in thinking
about the future is not to know what will happen, but
to be better able to think about what we might make
happen. Thinking about the future is important, therefore, because it provides a perspective on the present. It helps us to formulate more precisely and
concretely what we may reasonably hope for, anticipate, or expect.

In thinking about the future of community and school
relations, we shall need to formulate, therefore,
some judgments about what it may be reasonable to
expect. In doing so, it will be useful to distinguish
between what we might expect to happen and what we
might decide to make happen. We all recognize that
there is both change and continuity in history. If we
are to formulate judgments about the future, we must
first be particularly sensitive to those social forces
and social processes that are likely to extend into
the future and to provide a kind of continuous thread
with the past and the present. Having focused attention
on these underlying trends, we might then be in a
better position to assess the potentialities of interventions upon those forces in the relatively brief
period from now to 1990. The first focus, therefore,
must be upon what we may reasonably expect from
some important social forces already in process. The
second interest can then be to assess what we may
reasonably expect to result from stategies aimed at
influencing those forces. In what follows I am primarily concerned with the first of these interests--
the interest in what we might reasonably expect to
happen. I am only tangentially interested in the
second of these interests--what we may reasonably

expect to make happen.

A further distinction is in order concerning the topical focus of these relections. In thinking about the
future, we may forget that our aim is to formulate
reasonable judgments about what we may expect to
happen. Instead, there will be a tendency to discuss
what we would like to happen. I wish to keep these
two issues separated. I am not concerned with por-
traying what I think would be a good state of affairs
in the relations between schools and their communities. I am not concerned with setting forth what,
in my own judgment, would be a desirable course
of action. Neither am I concerned with devising a
strategy for change. I am concerned simply with
exploring the forces that are likely to persist no
matter what may be the future of school-community relations and only secondarily with assessing
current strategies in the light of these limitations.

Whatever it may be, the future of schools in relation
to communities will have to be described as a systemic relation between the profession, the public, and
the polity of education. By "policy" in this connection
I mean simply that set of institutions and social arrangements whereby power and authority are distributed, and within which debates on policy and procedures are carried on, and through which decisions
are implemented and enforced. At the level of the
nation, the polity would include that set of arrangements contained in the Constitution, together with
those arrangements for party organization that have
developed out of custom, together with other agencies established by statute through which policies
and procedures are formulated, evaluated, implemented, and enforced. Thus, the polity is not the

same as the government; not is it the people. It is
a set of institutions and social arrangements. It
would include the national conventions of the pol-
ical parties. It would not include the armed forces; but it would include the procedures for control
of the services and the institutional arrangements for
declaring war. Within education, the polity would
include some portions of the Federal Government,
the governments of the respective states, and local
boards of education. But increasingly, it also includes the professional associations of teachers
and academicians, local associations of parents,
student associations, and even publishing firms
and some agencies of industry. The polity of education distributes power and authority widely and
without much clarity.

The profession, the public, and the polity--these
are the three elements that must be contained in
any careful description of schools and communities
no matter what other changes may occur in American society in the future. Current school-community controversies demonstrate that the relations
between these three systemic elements are always
presupposed in the controversy. If the burning issue is how the lay public is to be given access to
control of the local school, then that issue can be
translated into a question about the relations of the
profession and the polity. What is a professional
decision in education, and what is a lay decision?
This question can be formulated by asking whether
the polity for the educational system should be
based in the profession or in the local community.
The question, "In what sense is the public school
public?" is simultaneously a question about the
authority of the professional, the structure of the

polity, and the role of the public. A satisfactory approach to the future of school-community relations ,must take account of all three elements. The principal difficulty in most conjectures about the future of schools and communities in America is that they tend to be developed from the point of view of the profession, or of the local public, or of the unquestioned social demands which a larger public places upon the schools.

Yet there is something peculiar about the current scene which would justify starting one place rather than another. It may be that today the most pressing issues of educational policy are incapable of formulation as issues of policy at all. They may be capable of formulation only as issues of policy. To adapt a phrase from George S. Counts, for the first time in this century the central question is not "Dare the schools build a new social order?" but "Dare the social order erect a new system of schools or a system of education without schools?" In other words, there is a sense in which the problems of education in our own day have to do not simply with what policies should be adopted by the educational system, but with what kind of system should be adopted within which to debate the questions of policy. When questions are raised concerning the very structure of the school system, the way authority is distributed within it, the role of the professional, the role of the community, and indeed the very purposes of schools, then clearly we are dealing with matters more fundamental than mere policy. We are dealing with problems of the policy for education. These are the hard issues that face us, and they have not received substantial treatment in the spite of volumes

Part III

on the future of education.

What, in the decades ahead, might be the points of
contact, the inter-relationship between the school
and the community? Consider the warfare out of
which the problem arises today. For the first time
in many years, practical proposals have been
made--and acted upon--which, though aimed at
the reform of urban schools, have been focused
on change in the control of local schools. There
is hardly anything local about either the power
or the accountability of local school bureaucra-
cies in such urban centers as New York City,
Chicago, or San Francisco. At the level of the local school, the relevant public, the local public,
is virtually disenfranchised. Within the neighborhoods or attendance districts of the local school,
there is, it seems, precious little that parents,
citizens, and friends of youth may do to influence
effectively, the way their children are educated.
More often than not, it seems the local concerned
public can only appeal to the representatives of
a larger and often unresponsive public to bring
about change. And in the process, the efforts
of the local public are deflected, diluted, and
rendered inconsequential. [2]

Alternately, the members of such a concerned
local public may appeal to the professional judgment of those who manage the school in its day-
to-day affairs. But the interests of the professional are all too seldom directed outward in a
concern for the hopes and fears of the lay public
and are all too often directed upward within the
bureaucratic structure of the school system. Thus,
it often seems that a local concerned public seeking some institutional avenue through which to ex-

press its interests in its children, can find no appropriate   local political body through which to act. The policy does not provide for it.

Proponents of reform therefore argue that a significant degree of effective control should be lodged directly in the community--in the local people nominally   served by the school. The argument so stated is excessively simplified, In the relations of school and community, it focuses on power, authority, and accountability. The argument is concentrated on the problem of control but, in the process, calls into question the relation between public, polity and profession.

This is the practical setting, then, of today's problem of contact between school and community. The problem has not always been framed in this way, nor is it the same everywhere even today. There was a time--and still are places--where the issues of school and community focused not on the contact between them, but on the independence of the school, its freedom from political interference, from narrow parochialism, and from regularization of practice and curriculum were the issues. Still, in most of our urban school systems, the problem of school and community is not the independence of the two, but the matter of how they can be usefully related.

These issues of community participation, professional autonomy, and government control are important since they characterize the polity for education. But I shall argue that they are not decisive. The fact that these issues arise, and the way in which they arise, is symptomatic rather than basic.

Part III

One must ask what it is that produces these symptoms and what forces might operate in the future
to change them. Only then will it be possible to clarify what we might reasonably expect to make happen. Making something happen can be viewed as an
act of intervention in some process or sequence of
events already underway. We can therefore ask two
questions. First, "What are the processes in which
we wish to intervene?" and secondly, "What form
might our intervention take?" The first question
is a matter of understanding how the "system" operates; the second is a matter of action upon the
"system." In what follows I am concerned primarily with the first of these questions--with the processes in relation to which action must be directed
and in the light of which the polity might be recon-
structed.

FIVE BASIC POINTS OF CHANGE
1. Specialization and Differentiation of Education

To what degree in the period 1980-1990 will education be viewed as institutionally specialized and
therefore differentiated from the broader pattern
of socialization? This is really an alternative way
of formulating one indicator of our question--How,
in the future, will school and community be related?
Forsaking all jargon of sociology, the question can
be formulated directly and simply. Imagine a visitor from a near plant. He wishes to understand, with
insight of an anthropologist, how our society works.
Among other things, he will want to find out where
education takes place, and so he asks. He will then
be interested in determining to what extent people
answer his question by pointing to a separate set

of institutions called schools. The degree to which
education is viewed as occurring in schools is evidence of the degree to which education is institutionally specialized and differentiated in the pattern of
socialization.

For over two hundred years the tendency in the West
has been toward increasing specialization, differentiation, and rationalization of institutions performing
fundamental social functions. In the case of education,
this tendency is evident in the steady shift from reliance on family, church, and shop as primary agencies of socialization to regularly established systems
of schools. The educative role of schools has expanded enormously until in this century we have come to
identify the education of the public with public schooling. The scope, size, and complexity of the American
"educational system" and the tendency to identify that
system with the school system is evidence of this
social tendency.

The process continues. Aid to education is aid to
schools. The question, "where did you get your education?" means "What schools did you attend?" An
expansion of education is clearly an expansion of
schools. Seldom is it asked how we might improve
our culture and more successfully transmit its
fundamental values from generation to generation.
That sort of question is invariably posed as a
problem of education, and is then immediately translated into a question about the improvement of
schools. Continuing institutional differentiation is
apparent also in the trend toward lay control of
ecclesiastically sponsored schools and colleges.
Education, in short, continues to become institutionally differentiated from the Church. And this
process, so evident in the growth of educational

institutions, is not confined to education. It is dis-
cernible also in the development of political and
economic institutions. It is not likely that such
forces will be reversed in education, strategic
though it is, without some accompanying change in
social structure elsewhere.

These observations are important because some efforts at educational reform are aimed at establishing new and more fruitful school-community relations and for full success would require at most a
reversal, but at least a redirection of this long
established and fundamental social process. For
example, even early in the New York controversy
over I.S. 201, the effort was partly intended to
nurture a community self-consciousness where it
had long been muted or ignored, and to relate the
school once again to the daily out-of-school processes of socialization based in the Harlem community. To do this required simultaneously an
attack on the polity and the professional roles in
the system. The ultimate intention is that our
interplanetary visitor should receive a different
answer to his question. "Where does education
occur?" Well, in the school, certainly, but also
on the street, in the neighborhood, and in lots of
other places besides. This answer can be viewed
as an intent to intervene in the process of institutional specialization and differentiation.

The question may be asked, however, whether such
efforts are aimed at reversing the trend or whether
they are aimed at advancing further differentiation.
It is possible to see the process of institutional
specialization along the following lines. The growth
of school systems has meant the progressive ex-

pansion of schools to encompass more and more of what, in the early years of the nation, was a function of other institutions or informal arrangements. When the family fails, the school must fill the gap. When industrial society renders it no longer possible to carry on education through an apprentice system, and factories become mis-educative environments, then the school must fill the gap. And so education becomes institutionally separated from the educative processes that go on elsewhere. Then compulsory attendance, joined with an extended period of schooling, means that children are under the care of the schools for more and more purposes over an increasing span of their lives. Furthermore, the growth of the school system simultaneously generates pressures for its regularization. Thus, associations of schoolmen emerge together with those rules, regulations, and procedures which create the polity, therefore generating and distributing authority-- always a central function of a polity. Suppose we take the view that this is the process by which education has become institutionally specialized and differentiated from the broader pattern of socialization. Then efforts at reform, such as I.S. 201 in New York, can be seen as aimed at reversing this process, or at least arresting it. The effort is to restore to the community, the family, and other informal associations their educative function and to limit the differentiated role of the school.

One could, however, take exactly the opposite view of the same target. The aim is not to reverse the direction of specialization, but to promote it, accelerate it, in order to limit the domain of the school's concerns. If schools became truly spe-

cialized and differentiated from other modes of socialization, then they would in fact concern themselves with only a small portion of the educative
process, while the remainder would be reserved
to the local communities, and their informal lay
organizations, libraries, playgrounds, museums,
and businesses. This sort of attack is seen from
time to time in our major cities. For example,
Ron Karenga, in Los Angeles, runs a community-
based educational program for blacks which is intended to supplement the regular schools, to make
explicit the limited nature of their program, and
to preserve a "black-consciousness" in the children. He is saying, among other things, that
there are some things the public schools can do,
but that they are not basic, not fundamental. He
would be satisfied, presumably, if those schools
were to become even more specialized than they
are now in order that they might be more limited
in their educational role and, consequently, so
that the local community might become more effective and establish its own complementary educational system.

These two approaches will produce different ideol-
ogies with respect to school-community relations.
But, strictly speaking, only the first is an effort
to improve and expand contacts between school and
community. The latter is aimed at minimizing
such contacts in order that the educative powers of
the local community can be developed through other
educative agencies. Both, however, appear to be
efforts at reversing the trend by which institutional
specialization and differentiation of education tends
to transform the school into a kind of total institution. Still, it seems reasonable to expect that these

efforts at intervention will remain essentially guer-
illa attempts. This is not to minimize their importance; nor is it even to suggest that they will fail.
It is only to suggest that they will probably fail to
become the prototype for American school systems
in general.

In respect to this judgment, there are two questions
one must ask. First, what are the underlying pressures in American society which lead to the specialization of education in schools and to their consequent differentiation from other institutions of
socialization? Secondly, to what extent can these
efforts at reform reasonably be expected to combat
those forces? These are difficult questions. They
can be answered only in a tentative and highly spec-
ulative way. It seems clear enough, however, that
institutional differentiation and specialization occur
because there is a particular social task that cannot be performed adequately with the available resources of time, attention, and money. The total
task of education, for example, is too important to
be entrusted to chance and too comprehensive to
permit individual families to give it the needed time
or effort. There must be some institution to carry
out this task so that men can turn their energies
to other things. Specialization occurs only if the
task of education is regarded as immensely important. Furthermore, it will occur only if education
is understood to require such sustained effort and
attention that it cannot be carried out in the normal
course of family life. Only if these two conditions
are satisfied will it seem apparent that the available
resources of effort and time are unequal to the task.
In that case, schools, or something like schools,
will be viewed as necessary. Differentiation and
specialization will take place.

Part III

Furthermore, if it is assumed, as it is widely assumed in modern societies, that   the execution
of certain social tasks requires not only sustained
attention but also specialized knowledge, then the
tendency is strengthened for schools to become increasingly differentiated and more inclusive in function. The educational system, at least in American society, is the only set of institutions whose
major function it is to produce the persons who will
man positions within the system. It is this function
based upon the assumption that specialized tasks
require specialized skills, which provides not only
the basis for the very concept of an educational
profession, but which simultaneously increases the
importance of schooling and strengthens the tendency
for schooling to become institutionally differentiated
from the rest of the process of socialization. If the
performance of specialized tasks requires special
skills, and if the conduct of education is an important and specialized task entrusted to schools, then
the authority to perform that task must itself be a
consequence of schooling.

The more it is assumed that education is important,
and the more it is assumed that its conduct requires
specialized knowledge and sustained attention, the
more will be the tendency for education to become
institutionally differentiated and specialized. I see
no reason to assume that any of these assumptions
will be successfully and widely abandoned in the
next fifteen years. Certainly there is no evidence
that education will be viewed as less important in
the years ahead. The trend seems to be altogether
in the opposite direction, and it seems not to be contradicted by any forces outside the educational
system. Neither is this trend questioned in the stra-

tegies for reform of school-community relations.
Indeed, both efforts at reform (that typified by developments in New York City and that represented
by the somewhat separist trend in Los Angeles)
presuppose that the institution of the school, in some
form, is not simply important, but decisive.

Neither does it seem possible to rebut successfully
the assumption that education is a comprehensive
task requiring more sustained effort than can be
expected from the informal, non-school life of the
community. If the denial of this assumption were
the direction of change, then the schools would not
be the locus of conflict. The direction of change
would not be to make the schools more "relevant, "
but to make them clearly and unquestionably irrelevant. Though some critics argue that the schools
are irrelevant, they do not usually make the point
as something to be encouraged. If they did, the
effort would be to replace the schools with something else altogether. This seems an unpromising
direction, however attractive the prospect may
seem to some social critics. It lacks promise as
a practical alternative because it calls for the formulation of a truly educative community, one in
which individuals universally see that the education of the young is a task requiring a major expenditure of time and energy on the part of each
member of the community. The creation of such
a community would, in itself, be a highly desirable goal to attain. But unless it is reached, the
discrepancy between the task of education and the
resources in time and effort available for its
successful performance would again become evident, and it would become necessary to reestablish
schools with their specialized tasks, their author-

ized leaders, and their institutionally differentiated roles. It also seems impossible to question the
proposition that specialized tasks require the employment of specialized knowledge and experience.
Certainly, this proposition cannot be questioned
in the case of educators unless it is also questioned
in the case of mechanics, carpenters, plumbers,
doctors, accountants, and a thousand other specialists.

What can be doubted, however, is that the particular specialization of knowledge, experience,
and fuction required for successful education is
presently represented by those who are authorized
to teach and direct the schools. It is important to be
as clear as possible on this point, for most efforts
at the reform of school-community relations are not
directed at getting rid of expertise where it is needed.
It is not doubted that specialized tasks require specialized knowledge for their performance. What is
being called into question is the way the educational
system identifies those who possess that specialized
knowledge. And since it is a characteristic function
of the educational system to produce those individuals who will man positions in the educational system, what is being questioned is the fashion in
which the polity of education distributes authority.
What is being questioned is the assumption that
the particular skills required for education are
themselves a result of experience in the educational
system. This does not destroy the basis for a profession of education, but it does hit at one way of
formulating the professional's claim to authority.

I have ventured the judgment that these changes,
even if successful, will not be enough to reverse

substantially the tendency of schools to become institutionally differentiated from the broader pattern
of socialization. The reasons for this judgment
should be apparent. The common strategies for reform do not question the value of formal education
itself, nor do they successfully question the need
for specialized institutions to carry out the task
of education. The power of the community to select
who will educate is not in itself enough to reverse
the tendency of the school to become an increasingly differentiated institution. Though it will do much
to improve the community's control over the execution of the school's tasks, it will, in itself, do nothing to redefine those tasks. And unless the next
step is taken, I see no reason to believe that schools
even under community control, will become less
specialized, less inclusive, exercising less control over the lives of children in a setting increasingly differentiated from the rest of the community.
A change in the locus of control will have the additional result of redefining the tasks of the school
only if an additional condition is met; namely, that
the members of the controlling community share
those values which would strongly tend to redefine
the tasks of the school. The important force in
change, then, is not that the community controls
the schools, nor even that it values education, but
that it values education for certain reasons or for
certain goods. The reasons for this last judgment
will be more clearly understood if we turn to our
next import locus for intervention.

2. The Predominant Values

What will be the prominent values that will tend to
shape the functions of the schools? In asking this

question, I am not raising the age-old issue of educational goals. Regardless of what goals educators articulate, one may still ask what are the actual social consequences of schooling. One may then ask what values are reflected in those consequences, and how those values provide the ideological support necessary to maintain those consequences. The values implicit in the consequences of schooling may or may not correspond to the intended and formally promulgated goals of educators. In order to render manageable this question of values, it will be convenient to employ a typology of alternatives.[3] These options are not meant to represent empirical generalizations drawn from actual school settings, but nonetheless, they capture some features of alternative values that might be used in defining the tasks of schools. Therefore, such a typology can be useful in formulating interesting conjectures about how conflicts between different sets of values might be expressed in educational policy and how they might be resolved in educational practice. The typology, then, is simply a conceptual tool useful in getting at our question. I shall simply set it down that the predominant values which support the functions of the school may be those of managerial education, traditional education, humanistic education, or religious education. These alternatives are not mutually exclusive in all respects, although they are in some. Nor would I claim that these types or their combinations are exhaustive. On the whole, they represent fairly discrete modes of emphasis rather than clear-cut alternatives.

By managerial education I mean that system of education in which schools are assessed primarily by the utility of their "product" to other institutions of society--most notably its economic and military institutions. I prefer to state the point in this fashion because of the values I want to emphasize here are most evident when we ask how schools are evaluated as opposed to particular individuals in the schools. I have argued elsewhere[4] that the contemporary American school is typically evaluated in relation to its "product." We have been unable to develop measures of educational output which are independent of input and which, therefore, clearly show results of the school. In short, if we select good students, we will get good graduates.[5] But the difficulty in distinguishing between input and output does not dissuade anyone from assessing schools in relation to their "product." From this point of view, the school is a productive enterprise, preparing people to take a functional role in an increasingly orderly, rational, and productive society.

When schools of a society are evaluated primarily by their ability to accomplish this complex set of tasks, then they are being evaluated by what I would refer to as managerial values. The appeal to managerial values is an appeal to the values of effectiveness and efficiency in meeting the demands of the society, as a whole, for educated manpower. But the managerial point of view is not confined to these points. It is also evident in the "factory metaphors" and "productive images" of the school itself. Teaching gets to be viewed as "making something happen"; as "managing the learning process"; as "producing a certain kind of person." Similarly, the counseling enterprise of the school gets viewed not as diagnostic, but as the educational equivalent of quality control.

Even more important is the fact that when the school

is viewed from a managerial point of view, its functions tend to be defined and its results measured
primarily against aggregate values rather than distributive values. By an aggregate value, I mean a
good to be maximized for society even though it may
not be maximized for each individual within the society. By a distributive value, I mean one which is
to be maximized for each individual, though not
necessarily for the society as a whole. For example, policies directed at increasing GNP at a fixed
annual rate would be based upon aggregate values.
Success is compatible with a decline in real income for some individual members of the population. However, policies aimed at a more equitable
distribution of economic goods are likely to be based
upon distributive values, and their success would be
compatible with a decline in rate of economic growth
for the society as a whole. By managerial education,
then, I mean that system of schools in which policy
tends to be formed by aggregate values and in which
the function of the schools is primarily to provide
functional human resources for other institutions,
primarily economic and military.

By traditional education I mean that system of education in which the primary function of schools is
to preserve a collective memory, a capacity for
social recollection. The function of schooling, in
short, is to preserve in the consciousness of the individual a link with the past, the present, and the
yet unborn. Hebrew Day Schools in America are
good examples of what I have in mind. Such school
systems are also common in Africa, and these same
values are currently being stressed in some inner-
city innovations in this country. Visit one of the
store-front Freedom Schools and see how central

is the task of establishing a sense of self-identity in each child as an Afro-American. It would not be too much to say with Richard Niebuhr that the function of schooling from this perspective is to propagate and preserve a form of henotheism. He says of this form of education:

Every participant in the group derives his value from his position in the enduring life of the community. Here he is related to an actuality that transcends his own, that continues to be, though he ceases to exist. He is dependent on it as it is not dependent on him. And this applies even more to his significance than to his existence. The community is not so much his great good as the source and center of all that is good--including his own value. [6]

Here education is understood as firmly based in some historical community. However, that kind of education, reflected in schooling, need not be rooted in the contemporary local community. Indeed, it can be based in a collective memory of a community that has no geographical expression whatever.

By humanistic education I mean that education in which the primary function of the schools is to cultivate the "independence" of each "individual" and to develop each person to the fullest. This is phraseology familiar to anyone who has spent much time in schools of education. Humanistic education, so described, is frequently articulated as an ideal; but for good reasons, it is seldom embodied in the actual conduct of schools. Obviously, the notion of developing each individual to the fullest of which he is capable is not, in itself, an attainable ideal. Nor does anyone really believe it in any unqualified way. Everyone knows that human beings are capable of all kinds of things, many of which no one would wish to develop, let alone develop to the fullest. The ideal needs to be modified, shaped, and limited by many moral considerations that are not in themselves part of the ideal. It is not surprising, therefore, that the ideal becomes severely modified in practice.

The concept of the "individual,"moreover, is not in itself independent of cultural specification. It is likely to change radically through history. The Greeks, for example, who were by no means ignorant of the value of humanistic education, nonetheless used the term idiotes(individual) in a denigrating sense, a fact preserved for our consciousness only in the etymologically related term, "idiot. " The important point about humanistic education, however, is that the ideal is typically based upon the possibility of finding in the individual and in society two "centers of value" and, by separating the two, to place the claims of the individual over and against those of society and above those of society. Needless to say, traditional education tends to give more weight than does managerial education to what I have called distributive values. But humanistic education is focused distinctly, if not exclusively, in distributive values.

By religious education I do not mean to refer simply to parochial schools or ecclesiastically controlled institutions of education. I mean it to refer rather to that type of education focused primarily upon the holy, that education which is centered upon an object which transcends the self and is invested with the marks of the Holy. The aim, then, is not to develop

a functional "product" to be assessed by its value
in relation to some other institutions of the society.
The object of religious education, so conceived, is
to nurture a form of consciousness in which the individual sees his relation to others as mediated by
The Holy. Such a view of religious education includes some parochial schools, but not all. Nor is
it limited to ecclesiastical institutions.

The applicability of such a view, its modernity,
can be seen perhaps in the following conjecture.
It seems to me extremely doubtful, if not downright
self-contradictory, that a society can ever exist
which is fully secularized. The changing function
of ecclesiastical institutions is only partial evidence
of secularization. It may not be the most fundamental
expression of secularization. What we must ask about
the traditional sacred-secular distinction is not what
might   be the future extent of secularization, but
rather, where might The Holy be located in the social
life of the people. The problem for religious education
then, is not to determine what may be the future scope
and extent of the secular, but what may be the itinerary
of The Holy. [7]   The study of the movement of The Holy,
then, becomes basic in the foundations of a distinct
value orientation for education in the future. And this
will be so, even though religious institutions, as we
know them, prove indeed to be as the flowers of the
field which die and are burned.

In view of these different, though by no means exclusive, educational types, it is possible to develop some
interesting conjectures about what might be the character of school-community relations in the period
of our interest. It seems to me likely that humanistic education will continue to provide the educators'
ideology, but that managerial education will continue

to represent the reality. That is to say, the most
likely development may be that educators will continue to place primary importance on distributive
values in explaining their efforts to themselves.
But when important issues are raised influencing
the structural relations between schools and communities, the aggregate values of managerial education are likely to prevail in their actions. So the
professional ideology is likely to be humanistic, but
the operational ideology is likely to be one of social
utility.

To say this is not to imply that educators in particular
are infected with hypocrisy or duplicity. It is, rather,
to stress that human affairs in general are infected.
It is simply to take seriously the tensions that exist
between ethics and politics, between what is good
and right and what is possible or fair. The point cannot be fully explored here. It may be worth observing,
however, that the ideology in relation to which men
interpret their behavior must provide a moral defense
for their actions, and that typically it must do so on
the basis of distributive values. That is to say, it
must provide some justification for behavior between
men as men. But policies must be formed not on
the basis of what is good for this or that particular
man, but on the basis of what is fair for men in general   for men on the whole. Policies necessarily,
and politics for the most part, must be based upon
aggregate concerns. That is why, though it may be
a sound moral dictum to maximize good, it may
nonetheless be a better political guide to act so as
to minimize evil. To say, then, that educators are
likely to explain their actions to one another in the
terms of humanistic education and to act on values
of managerial education is to say simply that, when

structural problems arise between schools and communities, they are likely to act on grounds appropriate
to issues of politics and policy rather than on grounds
appropriate to the moral defense of their behavior.

One of the reasons that the managerial mode of viewing
education is so powerful is simply that it is the point
of view most adaptable to issues of policy. But there
are other reasons. As far as I have been able to determine, it is simply an historical fact that no society
has ever succeeded in assessing the output of its educational system, except in relation to its input to some
other set of institutions. Indeed, it seems almost the
logically necessary minimum condition of a satisfactory educational system that it effectively provide for
the orderly functional preparation of people to assume
positions within the economic institutions of society.
The features of an educational system based entirely
upon humanistic values could be delineated by asking
whether it is possible to assess the results of education
entirely in terms of what it does for persons, and not
for its efficiency or its effectiveness to any other institutions. The possibility of doing this seems remote
indeed. The question at hand, then, is not whether the
managerial trend in American education will be abandoned. It will not. The question is whether and to what
extent it will predominate. It is my judgment that it is
more reasonable to expect it to predominate than it is
to expect it to decline in influence.

For example, it seems reasonable to believe that efforts
to solve the problems of ghetto education will continue
to provide the value support and sanction for the managerial trend in American public schools; the ghetto notion
that education is the modern form of patrimony will
strengthen this tendency even more. I am sure that this
judgment is not self-evident, particularly to those who are
familiar with the range and fundamental character of edu-

cational criticism to be found in the black community in general and among exponents of black power in particular. The charge is often made not simply that American schools have failed to successfully educate black children, but more importantly, that what is called successful education in the schools is in fact, not good education at all. Whereas a good education would be based on a traditional or humanistic model, what in fact happens is that education is aimed at making black people white. The criticism is precisely that what is "bad" about education in American schools is that it is managerial in intent. It is aimed at making "black" children fit "white" society.

I am personally sympathetic to this view. In my own judgment the criticism is valid, and that admission may seem to contradict my earlier judgment that the managerial trend in American education will continue to prevail. But what is it reasonable to expect? It may well be true, indeed I think it is true, that in the black ghettoes of our cities a kind of traditional education deeply rooted in the community and in social memory is an essential next step, and if the effort is successful it will have some impact on the reformulation of the purposes of education in all schools. But unless we envision the ultimate solution of our racial problems to be total separation, we cannot suppose that this effort is any more than essential phase.

Even today, I suspect, the majority of white Americans would hold the view that, if we could solve the racial aspects of school-community relations in one sudden sweep of change, that solution would be the most successful assimilation of our black population into so-called white American society. I suspect, moreover, that most blacks would agree. It is only because that total sweeping and sudden change is not possible that we can and must speak, in the meantime, of "black education" based upon a traditional or humanistic model. This is to acknowledge, however, that though the movement is important and will have its consequences it cannot be viewed as a prevailing type of education likely to persist through the next two decades.

Indeed, most of the rhetoric used in defining the "problem" of ghetto education is framed in traditionalistic and humanistic terms, but with clearly managerial aims in mind. Again, and again it is reiterated that the ultimate objective of the educational system in the ghetto setting is to provide the skills necessary for employment and survival in a demeaning environment. Though the means adopted are clearly traditionalistic and humanistic, the objectives are equally clearly managerial. It seems to me, therefore, that the reasonable expectation is that even if we can find the means to survive the next decade and the population is substantially younger, nonetheless, the managerial type of education will be strengthened. And though the humanistic and tradionalistic focus on education will also be strengthened for the generation of young people in the next five years, it will not be strengthened proportionately.

We can expect religious education or humanistic education to continue to be the theory espoused by the parochial systems of education, if they can survive to the year 1990. But these schools, like the schools of other ghettos, can, at best, differ only marginally from those provided by the State. Among other things, they must be prepared to equip students to enter other parts of the educational system. Indeed, that is a managerial consideration which operates as a constraint on all schools. Hence, we cannot expect the parochial schools to depart substantially from the managerial values which prevail in the rest of the educational system. That constraint is so fundamental that it means such schools must operate at the minimum on managerial values.

It seems to me, however, that there is a more far-reaching change likely to take place in the next twenty years which will influence these schools directly and will, in its consequences, support my contention that the managerial values will predominate in shaping the functions of education. We must recognize that the various parochial systems of schools are presently in the most serious financial crisis of their history. We must also recognize that in many localities they constitute a substantial segment of the total educational enterprise. Despite their private or ecclesiastical sponsorship, there can be no doubt that they serve a very substantial public function. Were they to close shop simultaneously and in toto, the size of their role would be evident in the crisis facing the public schools.

It is becoming increasingly evident in legislative action and in recent Supreme Court decisions concerning textbooks, that the principle of child benefit has been carried about as far as it can reasonably be pressed. [8] It seems to me extremely likely that within the next ten to fifteen years the child benifit theory supporting public aid to Church schools must be overturned in favor of a different legal doctrine which holds that, in providing public support for these schools, the government is aiding not the student, but the public function of such institutions. We may expect the view to become more widespread that the central function of schooling, regardless of its sponsorship, is public, and that we can no longer let schools be as bad as they can be. Neither can we afford the view that the purposes and consequences of education are private just because the sponsorship of schools is private. If this shift occurs toward some kind of "public benefit" principle, then parochial school systems will be able to receive public funds even more readily than they do now.

This change, however, will exact its cost. It will reduce even further the range of differences open to such schools. In effect, they will become public schools, on grounds, moreover, which will constitute a substantial reinforcement of aggregate values at the expense of the distributive values implicit in "child-benefit". I would not, therefore, expect the parochial schools to continue to 1990 in anything resembling their current role. They will, in all probability, approximate in practice more and more closely a managerial type of education, though in ideology they will doubtless remain the chief exponents of an increasingly rare form of religious education.

If, in the decade of the 70's, the stresses leading to social disorder become more serious, as they may, then there will surely be a tendency for "traditional" education to grow in importance. The danger of this trend is not in the notion of "traditional" education itself, but in the fact that, joined with civil tension, it may produce a widespread kind of jingoism which would be all the more dangerous to our political institutions because it could be defended in the name of those institutions. We are concerned here with assessing the plausibility of my original conjecture that we may reasonably expect "managerial" education rather than any other to prevail as we approach

1990. Surely, it seems reasonable that no wide-spread "jingoism" would be tolerated if it hindered the fulfillment of the managerial functions of the educational system, and that fact seems to support my conjecture.

But how likely is it that such a constraint will oper-ate effectively? Certainly, there seem to me no a priori reasons to suppose that even the most paro-chial nationalistic kind of "traditional" education would hinder our military institutions. It seem to me less clear, but certainly possible, that the ad-vancement of neither our technological capacities nor our economic institutions would be limited by such a "style" of education. Indeed, all things con-sidered, a kind of narrow jingoistic form of tra-ditional education is, of all other possibilities, the most likely alternative to the managerial mode of education.

If this seems an unduly pessimistic outlook, I would hasten to add that I am aware of other more san-guine projections. I am concerned, however, not with what I think is desirable or good, but with what seems most likely, barring any systematic intervention. I am aware, for example, of the view that "humanistic education" may well become the dominant tone of adult education, that cybernation and automation will necessarily lead to a new emphasis on education for leisure and therefore a switch toward "humanistic" education. But how likely is this more optimistic view?

There are three points that need elaboration. In the first place, I think one needs to ask why it is that adult education is so often viewed as the most likely prospect for developing a substantially different and

more "humanistic" form of education. Is it because
adult education is more likely to be education for
leisure? Is it because preparation for work, having
been completed, will now give way to preparation
for enjoyment? I would suggest a different set of
reasons. Adult education seems the most likely sec-
tor for the development of truly "humanistic" modes
of education because it is not taken seriously in our
society, because the concern is marginal, because
it is not involved in the serious business of our
central educational institutions. It is precisely this
marginality of adult education which leads me to
say it will probably not be influential in shaping the
dominant educational values of the next two decades.

The same premises, however, can lead to a different conclusion. Precisely because adult education,
in all its aspects, is marginal, detached from the
constraints of certification, degree-granting and
credit accumulation, precisely because adult education can be operated by a host of talented but
"unaccredited" people, it may prove to be the most
flexible and easily changed segment of the educational system. If the nation were to shift substantially
its resources from the "core" institutions of post-
secondary education to a new emphasis on the entire
range of adult education, the result quite conceivably
would be a substantial shift in the reasons for which
people seek educational experiences. And the direction of that shift could well be away from the managerial values which place so much importance on
degrees and certificates to the more humanistic interests which may be essential in the future.

It does not seem to me likely, however, that such a
massive redistribution of resources in the educational

system would be likely to receive much support in those quarters where educational policies and appropriations are currently made. Consequently, this path of development, though possible, seems not likely. The important point is that the marginal character of adult education is simultaneously what renders it unlikely as a significant point where change will occur and strategic as a point where substantial change could be made to occur.

In the second place, however, one must acknowledge that if we attain a true leisure society in which cybernation renders jobs obsolete, then indeed there would come a substantial revolution in all of education. But here again, I doubt that that revolution would come in the period before 1990, and I doubt even more that it would result in a form of "humanistic" education. In America, the problem of education for leisure is not that it would occur in a society without jobs, but that it would occur in a culture that insists on expressing the idea of leisure in categories appropriate only to work. Education for leisure is often phrased as education aimed at letting people "use their free-time profitably." The metaphor is absurd as an expression of leisure. In a society where the importance of jobs is decreased, and leisure is thought of as "free-time" or as time away from jobs, the solution may be to educate for work that is independent of employment. In short, education for leisure, in our kind of society, is most likely to be framed in images of effort and product, time spent and result. The underlying educational metaphors are likely to remain those of process and product as opposed to those of play and intrinsic enjoyment.[9] Even under the latter conditions, the basic values are likely to be those of managerial education.

I recognize that the increasing emphasis in an affluent society upon hedonistic satisfactions and
instant pleasures may well be a harbinger of things
to come. But this can be seen more accurately, I
think, as a search for meaningful work in a society
where work and job are viewed as synonymous. In
short, the advent of the leisure society certainly
does not mean that education for leisure will sud -
denly become modeled after the "humanistic" style
of education. It may mean simply the transfer of
"managerial" values to activities conducted away
from remunerative employment. One might argue
that the advent of a leisure society will at least
make it possible for the "humanistic" model of education to prevail. My own judgment is that it would
become possible only in the logical sense of "possible. " In fact, it would not render it more likely
at all.

Finally, we must recognize the latent consequence
if a truly leisure and affluent society were to emerge
in the next twenty years as a consequence of technological advance. If most projections on cybernation
are to believed--which is itself doubtful--what is
likely to result is not a society in which education
for leisure will predominate in a "humanistic"mode,
but one in which there is a very high level of managerial education for an elite, and a lower level of
managerial education for the majority.

All things considered, then, if we ask what, in a
surprise-free projection, we might reasonably expect to be the predominant values shaping the functions of the schools, then our answer will have to

be those aggregate values of the great society rather
than the distributive values of the good community.
The schools will probably continue to function to provide the human resources for the economic and military institutions of our society. They will probably
continue to be viewed as the productive institutions
they are, and the values that govern will be those
appropriate to such a productive enterprise. We
shall find this somewhat dismal prospect further
strengthened if we turn to our third question.

3. Conflict of Values: Credentialism and Pluralism

To what extent is there likely to be a compatibility
between the values embodied in the functions of the
schools and the fundamental values of the larger society? This question touches on a great many points
of importance to educators. It must be answered in
some forms, for example, if we are to understand
the extent to which schools can be reasonably charged
with the responsibility for changing values or leading
in any kind of social change. It must also be answered
if we are to understand the degree of pluralism per-
missible among schools. Moreover, however these
questions are answered, asking them will influence
directly the extent and nature of school-community
relations. For if the values embodied in the functions
of the school depart substantially or conflict with the
values of the rest of society, then the school in its
organization and conduct will necessarily have to maximize its independence from the community, and
this will tend to maximize its specialization and differentiation from other institutions of youth. In what
follows I shall be able to comment only on two aspects
of these important problems. The first is credentialism; the second is pluralism.

Let us return to an earlier question. Under what
social conditions would we expect school-community
relations to become a serious problem framed primarily in terms of control of local schools? What is
it, in short, that creates these problems of public,
polity, and profession in just this way? Christopher
Jencks once remarked that the single most successful hypothesis in explaining the structure and operation of large urban school systems would be that
they are organizations held together by mutual mis-
trust. That is why the reach of authority and control
must extend so thoroughly all the way from the sup-
erintendent to the classroom teacher. I do not wish
to assess the truth of this remark, but only to point
out the unquestioned realities to which it points. The
kind of authority that Jencks saw is characteristic
of certain kinds of bureaucratic organizations, and
it is an undoubted fact that in large urban systems,
bureaucratization and professionalization are among
the pre-eminent features of such schools. Let us
suppose further that these features of the school system have cut the local community off from any effective means of influencing the schools at the local
level. The polity provides no access to control of
the school on the part of the local community. In
that event, we might expect school-community relations to constitute a focus of serious conflict.

This conclusion, however, would be too hasty. Regardless of how effectively the local schools are
insulated from the local community, relations will
not be a serious point of contention on those grounds
alone. For example, if the schools are isolated
but generally acknowledged to be very successful,
then it is hard to imagine school-community relations to be a serious point of contention. To the

bureaucratization and professionalization of the
schools we would have to add another necessary
condition before we reach a point of serious controversy. That condition must be that the schools are
simultaneously both insulated from the community
and also unbelievably bad, or unsuccessful. One
cannot escape the impression, for example, that
if the schools in central and south Harlem or in
Roxbury were eminently successful in teaching
reading, mathematics, science, and, in general,
maintaining the interest of the children so that they
scored at grade level or above on standard achievement measures, then the problem of community
control of schools would not arise. The failure of
the schools must be counted a necessary condition
for these issues to arise.

Yet, even this conclusion would be too hasty. Neither
of these conditions, taken individually, is enough to
produce the problem in its contemporary form. Nor
are they jointly enough to do so. We must remember
that education can be bad, even very bad, and still
be benign.[10] For example, under conditions of massive and sustained unemployment, in which there are
no jobs for either the educated or the uneducated, the
quality of schooling makes little difference to one's
life chances outside of school. It is easy to imagine
other circumstances in which schooling can be very
badly done, the schools cut off from local influence,
and yet no points of contention will arise. Yet if
we add other circumstances to these conditions,
school-community relations become serious and even
explosive.

If we are to understand the contemporary problem
of school and community, we must add a third neces-

sary social condition. It is simply that the credentials awarded by the school are taken seriously by
institutions and publics outside the school. The educational system is granted increasing powers to al-
locate human beings to social roles. It is precisely
this condition which makes it impossible for bad
education to remain benign. Under conditions of sustained, widespread unemployment, such as I described, school credentials cannot be taken seriously;
and when schooling is regarded as irrelevant to out-
of-school performance, school credentials will not
be taken seriously. It is the case, in fact, that the
credentials, the school awards (diplomas, certificates, degrees, etc.) need not be relevant to any
social roles in the society. Indeed, there cannot,
in principle, be any necessary relation between the
specific skills certified in various school certificates
and the specific skills required for any particular
role in society, simply because there are no specific
skills certified in such credentials. Neither should
we suppose that the irrelevance of school credentials
to specific social roles is necessarily part of what
we mean by saying that education is bad. What is
important here is not that school-awarded credentials are relevant or irrelevant, but simply that
they are taken seriously as screening devices for
access to social roles and to subsequent education.
The creation of these conditions constitutes an intensive limitation on the scope of the polity of education
and strongly reinforces the managerial values underlying the system.

I have said nothing so far about the role of "white
racism" or "black separatism" in creating the contemporary problem of school-community relations.
Until recently, and indeed to a large extent still,

black Americans had every reason to view schooling
as members of a society in which massive and sustained unemployment was one of the facts of life. For
the most part, no matter how good their education,
it would probably have little impact on their life chances. Therefore, whether schooling was good or bad
made little difference to them. Now, however, opportunities are beginning to open more visibly both
within the black community and outside. Changes
outside the schools, in short, have made school credentials important and the quality of schooling decisive. Under these three conditions--the insulation
of the school management, the ineffectiveness of
schools, and the crucial importance of school cre-
dentials--the relation of school and community, especially in urban centers, becomes explosive. If
anyone of these conditions is changed, community-
school relations will not be so explosive. Furthermore, it is the combination of these three conditions which focuses the problem on power, control,
and accountability.

The changed role of credentialism is particularly
important in this process. There is no doubt, in my
mind, that our society is moving toward performance
rather than ascription as the criterion for status. But
what is peculiar in the process, and also unnecessary
and questionable, is the progressively closer identification of school credentials as the measure of past
and future performance. Under these conditions,
academic achievement--i.e., performance in schools--
becomes not simply a means of awarding social
status by achievement. On the contrary, academic
certification becomes the means of assigning status
by ascription--a form of meritocracy in which the
measure of merit is established by a peculiar kind

of achievement. This is what makes the schools so
decisive in the community.

Thus, the underlying issues in the relations of school
and community only superficially have to do with authority and control. They basically have to do with the
purposes of the schools and the meaning that should be
attached to the credentials they award. So far, the
most evident problems in the school-community relations, if solved, will not touch upon these underlying issues. School decentralization, local boards
in urban centers, educational parks on urban boun-
daries--all these measures, unless they simultaneously attack the metaphors of market and manu-
facture by which the schools are assessed, may well
strengthen the managerial values which it seems reasonable to believe will continue to shape the social
functions of the schools.

As I mentioned before, some of the most interesting
black criticism of the schools is directed precisely
at the issues of the purposes of the schools and the
meaning of their credentials. The so far small and
quiet efforts in certain places to teach Swahili and
African history are clearly not managerial in intent.
Indeed, the fact that they are not is sometimes given
as the reason why such efforts should not be encouraged.   But the point is that such efforts get a redef-
inition of the purposes of the schools and constitute
a reassessment of the meaning of their credentials.
To the extent that these efforts are successful, they
will change the fundamental values expressed through
some schools. For reasons already discussed, however, I would not expect these efforts to change the
total picture very much.

Part III

It seems to me, in short, that we cannot expect any
substantial incongruity to exist between the values
expressed in the functions of the schools and those
embodied in the larger society. As we move more
and more into an achievement society, we must expect the schools to function increasingly as the channel of access for manpower and a primary agency
to "fit" the human resources to the requirements of
technological and military institutions. Regardless
of whatever else they may do, the problems of ghetto
schools will be solved only when they perform these
"managerial" tasks well. They will be able to differ only marginally from other schools. This leads
to the next point--the likelihood of extensive pluralism.

Pluralism has meant at least two different things.
On the one hand, a pluralistic society is one whose
political decisions are forged out of the pressures,
counter-pressures, and cross-currents of opinion
that reflect a multiplicity of interests. This may be
called political pluralism. To the extent that politics, as opposed to some form of tyrannical rule,
is always the adjustment of conflicting interests
and powers, we would have to say that political pluralism is simply a necessary condition for the existence of politics. By a "pluralistic society" we
might also mean, however, one in which there are
available institutions through which people can give
concrete expression to a multiplicity of different,
even incompatible values. This might be called
value pluralism. Our interest is in this second form
of pluralism. [11]

Values, to have any concrete social reality, must
be made incarnate in social institutions, or in the

behavior of people who wish to embody them in institutions. It follows that value pluralism can occur
only under certain rather specific conditions. In the
first place, the society must contain institutions designed to permit, or even encourage, the expression
of different value commitments in specific behavior.
This means, in respect to schools, that a society
which takes value pluralism seriously would have to
provide not simply comprehensive schools making
available different curricula and different career
choices. Rather, the society must provide schools
based upon quite different interpretations of the function of schools, the social meaning of education, and
the importance of learning.

Not even this, however, is sufficient. Value pluralism
may be visible when a society is viewed in its entire-
ty. Yet the choices available in the society as a whole
may not be available to individuals within it. It has
been a fond boast of American educators that nothing
characterizes American education as much as diversity. No generalization is so secure as the one which
states that no generalization is possible, and every
conceivable kind of school can be found in America.
Yet this observation, though true of American schools
as a whole, is false for the vast majority of Americans.
Certainly it is not true for most children in the ghetto.
They know, on the whole, that they can choose but one
kind of school, and that in recent years it has been a
successful school. The second condition that must be
met in a value-pluralistic society is that alternative
value choices must be available not simply somewhere, but everywhere in the society. They must be
available to individuals.

It follows that such value choices must be available
to people of roughly equal legal status and approxi-

mately equal educational opportunity. These two conditions are necessary, because without them we would
have a society which is pluralistic only in an aggregate sense. Pluralism would be based on privilege,
and that is fundamentally a form of caste, not pluralism. Some steps have been taken, recently, to
meet these conditions at the level of higher education where some eastern colleges, formerly concerned with educating a relatively privileged class,
have taken steps to encourage the admission of "un-
derprivileged" (note the adjective) students who had
not previously applied and to adjust their program
accordingly. A degree of equality, equal access to
alternative value choices, is a third necessary condition for a value-pluralistic society. This condition currently is not very adequately met in the case
of elementary and secondary education.

There are two final conditions necessary for the maintenance of value pluralism. On the one hand, the
choices available to members of the society must be
fundamental enough to produce significant differences
between people in their attitudes and outlook on the
world. On the other hand, those differences must not
be so fundamental as to be divisive. When the value
choices, behaviorally expressed, are not regarded
as very important in their consequences, then we have
not pluralism, but a form of indifference, to fundamental values. But when the differences between people in values, attitudes, and outlook, become divisive
we do not have pluralism either. For example, we
would not normally regard the aims of French separatism in Canada as a tendency toward pluralism,
nor would black separatism in this country, if successful, add to a pluralistic society. It would exa-
cerbate an already divided society.

Except under rather special circumstances, it seems
to me impossible to maintain value pluralism in a
society committed to mass education of a managerial
type. Any attempt to meet the condition of equal access, for example, will tend to place a heavy burden
on the schools for "traditional education " under the
rubric of "civic" education and that will tend to
counteract efforts to differentiate schooling, producing instead a kind of bland tolerance of value differences which denies that they represent anything
serious. This will lead, in fact has already led, to
a fundamental and widespread misunderstanding of
the educative value of conflict.

Moreover, if mass education and the society itself
are technologically oriented, then the first, third,
and last conditions will tend not to be met, because
the utilization of technology, its management and production, inherently require the adoption of certain
limiting modes of behavior, certain attitudes toward
time, the manipulation of things and people, toward
nature and toward social organization itself. In short,
the behavior required for "doing well" in such a society is simply incompatible with a great many options
of value commitment behaviorally expressed. A full
and detailed exposition of the point would show that
the conditions necessary for a full flowering of value
pluralism are probably not possible in a society whose
educational system is based upon the manpower ideology and aggregate values of managerial education.

To alter this situation and create true value pluralism
would require a massive commitment of our society
to "humanistic education, " a corresponding change
in the allocation of resources to and within education,
and a substantial shift in the structure of educational

authority, the social roles of teachers, and the means
of assessing the accomplishments and the purposes of
schools. These changes, it seems to me, could come
only by abandoning some aspects of the goal of mass
education, by establishing genuinely pluralistic school
systems instead of merely "comprehensive" schools
and by simultaneously redistributing the certification
function of the schools to other institutions so as to
permit free and random entry and exit from the educational system and to modify the functions of the
schools.

It seems unlikely to me that these changes will occur.
If they do not, then it seems reasonable to expect that
managerial education will continue to provide the values that move the schools, only marginal differences
between schools will be permitted, and the unlikelihood
of value pluralism will mean that the schools will be
in a difficult position to act as the initiating agency for
any significant change in social values.

On the other hand, we can get some foretaste of the
shape such developments might take if they do occur.
It could happen that state authorities will begin operating schools in direct competition with local school
boards. Public assistance in many forms might be
provided industry to expand training programs into
full-fledged schools. The movement of "teacher militancy" may well provide strong incentives for this
development. Or we may see local and state authorities
contracting with private, even ecclesiastical, corporations to provide specific educational services on a
large scale. Finally, within the period of our concern,
I would expect large inequities in per-pupil expenditures within states to be declared unconstitutional.
One form in which the resulting problems could be

met would be to provide tax funds for tuition payments instead of taxation for public schools.

Any of these developments would tend to enlarge the possibilities for value pluralism expressed through educational institutions, but the last, in particular, would have a substantial impact in that direction. Oddly enough, it seems also the least likely of these developments. It would seriously modify the polity of education, relate it more directly to the local community, and as a consequence, substantially change the current ideology by which the role of the professional tends to be defined. Aside from some such fundamental alteration in the polity of education, I see little possibility for a shift away from the managerial values of the system, little possibility of genuine value pluralism, and consequently, little possibility for more than small, local, and temporary success in the continuing effort to change the typical insulation of the school from the community.

4. Differential Rates of Change

A more complete treatment of the school-community problem would have to include some judgments about the different rates of change it would be reasonable to expect among various sectors of our society. Differing speeds of change, under certain conditions, could lead to stress which would revive the demand for "traditional" education and alter the picture considerably. The question cannot be given the detailed treatment it deserves within the limits of these reflections. In general, however, it seems to me true that educational forecasts, as contrasted with technological forecasts, are likely to be faulted not by underestimating the rate of basic change, but by overestimating it.

There is profound stability, perhaps inertia, in the process of education and in educational institutions. Changes of any basic sort take a long time. They take even longer to be recognized. It seems to me that, unless there occur such fundamental changes in the polity of education as to produce a radically plural- istic "system," the rate of change in education will continue to be much slower than in the rest of so- ciety. The result could be a serious strain on the social fabric, with consequences extremely difficult to anticipate in detail. Indeed, it seems reasonable to expect that, if between the educational system and the rest of society, the differences in the rates of change are sizeable, then many unexpected things may happen, things which would substantially depart from the picture of the future set forth in these re- flections.

5. Educational Technology

These remarks have not included any serious men- tion of the long run impact of educational technology. This omission is important and intentional. It is based upon some basic convictions about the way edu- cational technology influences the character of edu- cation and the forces required for its widespread adoption. In general, the most reasonable expecta- tion seems to be that up to 1990 the adoption of tech- nology within education will be somewhat slower than it is outside of education. Educational technology is often seen as a force for change endogenous to the "system." That is to say, the spread of educational technology is often seen as a social force for change on a par with the underlying pressures for differen-

tiation and secularization that we have already discussed. What is often forgotten is the fact that, in
thinking about the future of schools, it is not nearly
as important to consider the attainable technology
as it is to consider the social and institutional changes that will be necessary if that technology is to be
widely adopted. These underlying forces are the
matters that need primary attention in assessing
the importance of educational technology.

In general, Americans have not adopted technological
innovations simply because they are available. They
have embraced them only when it has become socially
advantageous, economically profitable, or politcally
necessary. For example, it may well be that educational technology in all its forms will be given its
greatest impetus by such a rapid increase in teacher
salaries that a substitute for the teacher becomes
politically and economically necessary. Thus, teacher
militancy may be a stronger force for the adoption of
educational technology than anything that media specialists or the reformers may do. Similar hypotheses
may be developed to indicate the social constraints
against the adoption of educational technology. Thus,
the omission of serious concern with educational
technology reflects the conviction that, with respect
to the future of schools, the technology of education
can be viewed as an exogenous force. The more important focus of attention must be upon those underlying social processes which will shape the relation
between school and community and provide either a
fertile field or a barren field for the spread of technology in education. One cannot avoid the impression
that the development of space technology would not
have occurred as a consequence of technology itself.

It needed an explicit decision of national policy.
And that too would not have taken place independently of the peculiar relations between the United
States and the Soviet Union. The technological revolution is upon us, and it will spread to education.
But it will probably not spread as a force for substantial change in education unless some other basic changes make it necessary.

Conclusion

That we live in an age of change is, by now, an observation so often repeated that one hesitates even
to mention it. The only certainty about the future is
that it will be different. And so, we must learn to
educate for change. Change is the only inevitability
in history. In the light of these common claims, it
may seem odd that reflections on the future of school
and community relations should anticipate so little
change. But change is not the only inevitability of
history. There is also continuity. There are forces
which tend to preserve a traceable thread between
the past and the future. I have been concerned here
with emphasizing those durable continuities, because
they are so often ignored. It may seem odd also that
these reflections contain so little in the way of for-
tunate visions of the future. But I have been concerned
not with developing what we may hope or desire to
make happen in the future, but with examining the
limits within which a reasonable hope might be framed
for a rather specific period of time. The challenge
is not new. It is not to accept this rather bland and
dismal picture of the future, but to make something
else happen, to shape a future which is more hopeful.

The most fundamental changes that we might·make

happen in the period 1980 to 1990 are those that re-
shape the polity of American schools and redefine
their purposes to reflect a national commitment
less managerial in intent. We may conclude with
our original theme. The central question is not
"Dare the schools build a new social order ?" They
probably will not; they probably cannot; and indeed,
they probably never could. The significant question
is "Dare the social order build a new system of
schools?" The answer to that question is problem-
atic but at least it is the right question.

Thomas F. Green is Director of the Educational
Policy Research Center at Syracuse University.

Notes and References

1. Strictly speaking, these are not judgments about
the future so much as they are judgments about certain intractable elements in the nature of human af-
fairs--past and future.
2. This point has been extensively explored in an unpublished paper prepared for the Educational Policy
Research Center at Syracuse by Professor Gerald
Reagan of Syracuse University.
3. To the best of my recollection, I first encountered
the categories used in this typology in an unpublished
paper entitled The Future as Incredulity by Manfred
Stanley, produced for the Educational Policy Research
Center at Syracuse.
4. See Thomas F. Green, Work, Leisure and the American Schools (New York: Random House, 1968).
5. I am tempted to add the phrase "no matter what the
school may do. "
6. Richard Niebuhr, Radical Monotheism and Western
Culture (New York: Harper, 1962).

Part III

Notes and References (cont'd)

7. Note the following distinction viewed from within
the prophetic tradition of the Old Testament. There
is a difference between The Holy and that to which
men relate as though it were holy. To anticipate
the movement of the former is an art not of scholars,
but of prophets. To anticipate the movement of the
latter is to deal with man's idolatries. It is to deal
with the functional equivalent of The Holy. That men
will persist in idolatry seems beyond doubt, and
that education can be rooted in such idolatries
seems also beyond doubt, even in a so-called "secular" society.
8. By the "child benefit" principle I mean that
fiction of the courts that, in permitting aid to
private schools through public funds, the state is
aiding not the institution, but the child.
9. I have attempted to develop the intricacies of
these arguments more completely in Work, Leisure
and the American Schools (New York: Random House 1968
10. This is a simple, but often unnoticed observation
that I owe to my colleague Professor Gerald Reagan, op. ci
11. The following discussion of the conditions for pluralism has been more fully developed in Thomas F. Green,
Education and Pluralism: Ideal and Reality, Twenty-
sixth Annual J. Richard Street Lecture (Syracuse University School of Education, 1966).

A Concept of School in 2000 A.D.

The following is excerpted from a working paper
prepared for the White House Conference on
Children by a group headed by John I. Goodlad.

THE RIGHT TO LEARN IS THE GOAL   WE SET
FOR THE 21ST CENTURY.

In a nation that speaks of inalienable rights, the
right to learn must be paramount. Yet that right, in
its full meaning, has been denied to many in this
nation. It has been denied because of color and religion, because of poverty and infirmity, and because
of place of abode. And it has been denied because of
our mindless adherence to unproductive teaching
concepts and practices.

The right to learn is the goal we set for the 21st
century. We want for our children a range of learning opportunities as broad as the unknown range of
their talents--and a learning environment that nurtures
those talents. We want them to have freedom, and
the order, justice, and peace that the preservation
of their freedom demands.

Yet we scarcely know the meaning of these grand
words, let alone how to give them body and substance.
Clearly, then, we must engage in great experiments
encouraging alternatives and diversity throughout what
must become a much more varied and comprehensive

educational system. This must involve: 1) the reconstruction of existing schools, 2) the creation
of new schools free of the present system, and
3) above all, the expansion of "school" into the
world.

A NARROW CONCEPT

Schools and teachers have been with us for so long
that we now equate them with education and, worse,
with learning. The infant learns to walk and to talk,
to trust and to distrust; he learns fear and love and
hate--all without benefit of school. The tragic irony
is that we know all this and still equate learning with
school. By age 5, the child has sat before a television set for at least the number of hours he will
spend in the first three grades of school. And still
we equate learning with school.

The first difficult step toward achieving our goal
is acceptance of what should be obvious: School
is but a part of the learning environment. Until recently, we believed that it was the most powerful
part of that environment; we know now that it is not.

We have only begun to question the outworn notion
that certain subjects or concepts are to be learned
by all individuals, at successive stages of growth,
at stipulated times, in sterile places. Reading is
for the first grade, long division for the fourth,
and fractions for the fifth and sixth. All this takes
place between the hours of 9 and 3 in a big box
divided into cells.

In this lockstep, as in so many other ways we teach
that each phase of life is instrumental to the next,
rather than of ultimate value in itself. We see the

man we want the child to become rather than the
child seeking to become himself. In the words of
Hannah Arendt, "Man sees wood in every tree."
Perhaps this is one reason why more than half of
all Americans over 50 say that they find their lives
to be disappointing, unrewarding, unfulfilling, and
find, when they come to die, that they "never had
lived at all."

This is the winter of our educational discontent. Until recently, we believed that we had only to inject
some new subject matter here, a heavier dose of
phonics there, tighten the discipline a little, to improve both the system and society. Better schools
(defined largely in quantitative terms) would mean
more jobs, a brisker economy, safer cities, and
more aware and dedicated citizens.

Or so we thought. Dwindling confidence in these
relationships reflects both declining confidence in
the schools and the tenacity with which we cling to
the "learning equals schools" equation. Painfully,
we are coming to realize that grades predict grades,
but is not a guarantee of good workers, committed
citizens, happy mothers and fathers, or compas-
sionate human beings.

For a brief span of years, we believed that the
sickness spread only through the schools of our
great cities. Increasingly, however, we have come
to understand that suburban and, to an even greater
degree, rural schools do not assure the diet nor
provide the vitality our children deserve. Even the
middle-class school around the corner reveals rag-
ged edges surrounding a soft center. The overall
failure is glaringly apparent in dropout rates, in

barely minimal learning on the part of the many who
do remain in school, and in growing alienation among
the young of all colors and classes.

WINNERS AND LOSERS

At the root of the problem is an implicit denial of
diversity. The schools have become great sorting
machines, labeling and certifying those who presumably will be winners and losers as adults. The
winners are disproportionately white and affluent;
the losers, too often, poor and brown or black or
red.

But many of the winners are losers, too. For they
are shaped, directed, and judged according to a
narrow conception of what is proper. This process
begins very early; the environment of expectations,
rewards, and punishments is established before
mother and child leave the hospital, and in the home,
infants are encouraged in their efforts to walk and
talk, but their responses to sound, color, and
smell are ignored or stifled.

The process of channeling energy and talent is re-
fined and perfected in the schools through a network
of expectations, rules, grades, required subjects,
and rewards for what is wanted and the subtle extinction of the great range of talents and achieve-
ments that are not wanted.

A massive task of change lies ahead. We cannot
point pridefully at those who have "made it" while
half of us believe that life has passed us by.

Among many of our people there is a sense of outrage induced by the discrepancy between what is

and what could be. We (the committee) share that outrage, but we have more than a little hope that a new era can be both described and created. At the core of this hope is a fresh awareness of child- ren --of their intrinsic rather than instrumental value, of their ability to learn, and of the kind of learning they could and should have going into the 21st century.

Other generations believed that they had the lux- ury of preparing their children to live in a society similar to their own. Ours is the first generation to have achieved the Socratic wisdom of knowing that we do not know the world in which our child- ren will live.

All that we can predict with certainty is that the central issue of the 21st century, as it is of this one, will be the struggle to assert truly human values and to achieve their ascendancy in a mass, technological society. It will be the struggle to place man in a healthy relationship with his natur- al environment; to place him in command of, rath- er than subservient to, the wondrous technology he is creating, and to give him the breadth and depth of understanding which can result in the for- mation of a world culture, embracing and nurtur- ing within its transcending characteristics the diverse cultures of the world of today.

The education of the 21st century man is necessar- ily an enabling process rather than an instruction- al one. It requires opening the whole of the world to the learner and giving him easy access to that world. This implies enormous respect for the child's capacity to learn, and with the granting of

respect goes, by implication, the granting of freedom.

LEARNING AS AN END

When we look to education in the century to come,
we see learning not as a means to some end but as
an end in itself. Education will not be an imitation
of life, but life examined and enjoyed. A prescribed
age for beginning to learn--or for ceasing to learn--
will be meaningless. So will age as a criterion for
determining what needs to be learned. And so will
the standard school day and academic year.

Compulsory education--or compulsory attendance,
as it might better be called--will be a thing of the
past. School as we know it will have been replaced
by a diffuse learning environment involving homes,
parks, public buildings, museums, business offices,
and guidance centers. Many such resources that are
now unofficial, unrecognized, unstructured, or un-
supervised--and unused--will be endorsed and
made fully available for learning. There will be
successors to our present schools--places designed
for people to gather for purposes of learning things
together.

Children and their families will be responsible for
setting educational goals and mapping the route toward them. Plentiful assistance and advice will be
available, if desired, in planning highly flexible and
individualized schemes for learning, but it will be
left to the learner--and, when he is very young,
his family--to choose among alternatives.

The very availability of a great range of options will

represent what we believe will be an important and essential change in our national value system. "Success" will have been redefined, and a wide range of studies, tastes, careers, and "lifestyles" will be legitimized and praiseworthy. Boys will not be made to feel that they must grow up to be aggressive--or even affluent--men. Girls will not need to feel that domesticity is the necessary be-all and end-all of their existence; a career in science will not have higher status than a career in the creative arts. We will, in short, give substance to our longstanding but never fulfilled commitment to honor and develop the entire range of human talent.

Modern technology will help us realize our goals. The profound significance of the computer, when properly used in learning, is that it introduces an entirely new source of energy into the educational process. It is energy that is not affected by the night before, by viruses or by unmanageable children. Subjects missed this year can be picked up next year. Single subjects can be pursued intensively for periods of time governed only by the whim of the learner.

It is possible that advanced technology will return the family to center stage as the basic learning unit. Each home could become a school, in effect, connected via an electronic console to a central educational computer system, a computer-regulated videotape and microfilm library and a national educational television network. Whether at home or elsewhere, each student will have, at the touch of a button, access to a comprehensive "learning package," including printed lessons, experiments to be performed, recorded information, videotaped lectures, and films.

The moment so much teaching energy is made available throughout the 24-hour span of the day to all individuals at any place, school need no longer be what we have known it to be. It may be used for other functions not fully recognized until now. It will be the place where human beings come together not for the formalities of learning subject matter but for the higher literacy going far beyond reading, writing, and arithmetic.

Heavier stress will be laid on learning different forms of rationality and logic and on dealing with crisis and conflict. The individual will be helped to develop a greater consciousness of his thoughts and feelings, so that he may feel and experience life and at the same time "stand outside" his immediate experience. For 21st century man would be a sentient being with both the freedom that comes from understanding and the accompanying control of impulse.

In such an educational world, everyone will be, from time to time, both teacher and learner, but there will still be great need for teachers who, for the first time, will be free to engage in truly human tasks. No longer will they need to function as ineffective machines, imparting "facts" by rote--real machines will have taken over that function. Some will spend many hours preparing a single lesson to be viewed by thousands or even millions of individuals of all ages; others will evaluate such counseling centers. Others will be engaging with groups of all ages in dialogue designed to enhance human communication and understanding.

The entire educational enterprise will be directed

toward increasing the freedom and the power of the
individual to shape himself, to live at ease in his
community and in doing so, to experience self-fulfillment.

ACHIEVING UTOPIA

We have sketched a kind of learning Utopia; achieving
it will not be easy. In fact, without massive, thoughtful social reconstruction, we will not get there at all.
To stand aside--unconcerned, uncommitted, and un-
resolved--may very well be to assure no 21st century
and, least of all, no Utopia.

The first step is moral commitment. Like all moral
commitments, it must be backed by resources and
action. We sound a special call for full and genuine
commitment to the right to learn.

The signal announcing this commitment will be the
long-awaited injection of large-scale government
funds into learning: for encouraging experimentation
in existing schools, for the creation of experimental
schools, and for transcending the schools by bringing
new learning into them and taking children to the
range of resources outside them. For a time, at
least, we must infuse these funds as though we were
at war--because we are at war--with ignorance, prejudice, injustice, intolerance, and all those forces
crippling and restricting young and old alike.

The first phase of reconstruction involves the schools
we have. Supposedly, the decade of the Sixties was
one of school reform: in the curriculum, in the organization of school classroom, and in instruction.
But recent studies reveal that the appearance of

change far outruns the actuality of it.

Despite emphasis on the need for identifying goals,
few schools have a clear sense of direction. Despite
the obvious futility of "teaching" the world's knowledge, schools still emphasize the learning of facts
rather than how to learn.

Despite this golden era of instructional materials
and children's literature, the textbook is still the
prime medium of instruction. Despite gaining knowledge about individual differences in learning,what
children are to learn is still laid out by grades,
years, months, and even days. Despite increased
insight into how learning occurs, teaching is still
largely telling and questioning. In a diverse, complex society, our schools demonstrate almost monolithic conformity and enormous resistance to
change; close scrutiny reveals a deep-seated im-
potence, an inability to come to grips with the acknowledged problems.

INVESTING IN THE UNKNOWN

The top agenda item, then, in seeking to enhance
learning in the Seventies is unshackling the schools.
The process must begin by decentralizing authority
and responsibility for instructional decision making
to individual schools. Simply dividing large school
districts into smaller districts is not the answer.
Schools, like individuals, are different: in size,
problems, clientele, and types of communities
served. They must create programs appropriate
to their local circumstances. Many schools are
not ready to take quick advantage of such sudden
freedoms. Too long fettered by the larger system,

their staffs will be timid and uncertain.

We recommend, therefore, that substantial federal funds be allocated for the deliberate development of schools whose sole reason for being is experimental. Designed to provide alternatives, such schools could provide options in the community and thus would attract a more supportive parent group. In time, such schools would provide models, for replication in networks of cooperating schools seeking to learn from each other.

Such schools need not arise solely within "the system." The need to break out of established patterns has never been more critical. We need alternatives wherever we can find them. Some of the "free" schools springing up around the country offer diversity and should be encouraged to the point where their practices truly reflect their underlying philosophies.

We urge that schools be given support for abolishing the grade levels, developing new evaluation procedures, using the full range of community resources for learning, automating certain kinds of learning, exploring instructional techniques for developing self-awareness and creative thinking, rescheduling the school year, and more. Most of all, we urge substantial financial support for schools, seeking to redesign their entire learning environment, from the curriculum through the structure of the school to completely new instructional procedures.

Especially needed are well-developed models of early learning. We know now that the first five years of life largely determine the characteristics of the young adult. Yet we fail these years shamefully

either through neglect, through narrow, thoughtless
shaping, or through erratic shifts from too little
to too much concern.

Two successive administrations have promised and
failed to deliver on a national effort for expansion
and improvement in the education of young children.
A National Laboratory in Early Childhood Education
suffered a crippled birth under one administration
and is now starving to death under another. We need
research on what we now know; we need thousands
of adequately prepared teachers to staff nursery and
play schools, and we need exemplary models of programs stressing cognitive, esthetic, motor, and af-
fective development.

REMAKING OUR TEACHERS

High on our list of "old business" is the overhaul of
teacher education from top to bottom. The continuing
debate over the value of "methods" courses, whether
to have more or fewer of them, and how to regulate
teacher education by legislative fiat only reveals the
poverty of our approaches to the problem. Shuffling
courses about is not the answer. Required are strategies that take account of the fact that preservice
teacher education, inservice teacher education, and
the schools themselves are dependent, interrelated,
and interacting components of one social system.

It becomes apparent, therefore, that financial resources must be directed toward those strategies
that link schools seeking to change with teacher education institutions seeking to shake out of established
patterns. The teacher for tomorrow's learning must
be prepared in school settings endeavoring to create
a new kind of tomorrow; most of today's teachers are

prepared for yesterday's schools.

The tasks for the Seventies may not have the heady
appeal of the slogans for the Sixties, but they have a
meaty substance about them, an "action" appeal for
students, teachers, parents, private foundations, and
all levels of government.

But we need not wait for the 1980's to get a good start
on other components of our visions for 2000. In fact,
some roots already are taking hold.

School, however reformed, is but one of the child's
resources for learning. Children spend more time,
perhaps learn more, for better or for worse, in the
electronic embrace of television. Television, however,
is but one of several powerful teachers of the electronic genre. The computer has even greater potential
because of its ability to coordinate an array of devices
for sight, sound, touch, and even smell.

We must stop talking about the possibilities and engage in experimentation on a much broader scale. To
date, educational television has teetered on the brink
of disaster, its limp fare failing to compete with commercial products, especially advertising. "Sesame
Street" demonstrates vigorously that this need not
be. It also demonstrates that successful use of television for desirable learning by children requires
substantial financial backing--for air time, for production, for evaluation, and especially for research
into what constitutes appropriate subject matter.
Ten years from now, initial use of television will
probably appear primitive.

One of the major tasks involved in bringing elec-
tronics productively into children's learning in-

volves a kind of research; namely, determining appropriate roles for human and machine teachers. The cant of audiovisual education insists that equipment be only an extension of human teachers. For computers, for example, to be mere aids of human teachers is to cripple both. We must recognize the fact that electronic devices constitute a new kind of instructional energy--indefatigable, relatively immune to changes in the weather, and contemptuous of time of day or day of week.

The human teacher, on the other hand, is sharply limited in energy pattern, highly susceptible to chills, immobile in times of flood and snow, and sensitive to time of day. Clearly, the tasks for human and machine teachers should be both differentiated and complementary.

When we come to recognize fully the characteristics and possibilities of electronic energy, most of the "givens" of schooling collapse. Learning need not take place in a box, from 9 to 3 each day, five days a week, 180 days per year. There need not be a school beginning at age 5, a graded school, or a "balance" of subjects throughout the day. Nothing need be "missed" because of absence, for it can be picked up tomorrow by asking the machine to retrieve whatever is wanted.

Experimentation is needed, beginning now and continuing unabated into the 21st century, to create and legitimize options for schooling. Soon it will be common practice to show a variety of cassette tapes through a home television set. Cable television promises a new set of options. And just behind both of these developments lies the home

computer television terminal plugged into several
video outlets, capable of playing its own records,
and cassettes, and providing printouts of the learning and cultural options currently available in the
community. Taking advantage of these alternatives
must be accepted and encouraged.

One way for us to begin to grow accustomed to
this nonschool freedom is to use the learning resources outside school much more vigorously.
Children should be excused from school for blocks
of time to gain access to a nonschool teacher, to
serve as apprentice to an artisan, or to practice
a hobby in depth.

THE ROLE OF DRUGS

We had better begin now, because we will need
all our imagination and wisdom to cope with some
of the critical moral questions soon to be thrust
upon us. We do know that drugs are being used deliberately, under medical supervision, to intervene in the learning processes of children. Electronic means are being used to assist in the treatment of childhood disorders. Independent of these
activities, drug use, ranging from mild exploration to dangerous abuse, is now a fact of life. Who
are to be judged deviant and needful of chemical
or electronic treatment? What restraints are to
be placed upon the use of drugs for educational,
self-serving, or destructive purposes?

And who is to make what decisions for whom? That
question is probably the most pressing educational
question for both today and tomorrow. It is at the
core of current discussions of accountability, vouch-

er   systems, and the like in schooling. It is at
the core of any minority group demands for self-
determination and equality. Ultimately, it brings
us into the matter of who owns the child and who
is to determine his freedom. To return where we
began, the right to learn means the freedom of each
individual to learn what he needs in his own way and
at his own rate, in his own place and time.

This interpretation of the right to learn will not be
easily understood. Nor are we likely to come
easily to full acceptance and support of the flexibility
and experimentation required to design the future of
learning. We urge our leaders at all levels to work
toward public understanding and support. We recommend that celebration of this nation's 200th
birthday in 1976 be taken as the occasion for a
nationwide dialogue about, and assessment of,
our entire learning enterprise.

John I. Goodlad is Dean of the Graduate School of
Education, University of California at Los Angeles.

The Impending Instruction Revolution

Harold E. Mitzel

I PREDICT THAT THE IMPENDING INSTRUCTION
REVOLUTION WILL SHORTLY BYPASS THE SIMPLE
IDEA OF INDIVIDUALIZING INSTRUCTION AND MOVE
AHEAD TO THE MORE SOPHISTICATED NOTION OF
PROVIDING ADAPTIVE EDUCATION.....

First, let me explain my choice of the above titles.
It is fashionable in these days of rhetorical excess
to describe change as revolutionary in scope. The
mass media remind us daily that revolutions are
occurring right under our noses. We hear of (and
see) the Social Revolution, the Sexual Revolution,
the Technology Revolution, the Student Revolt, the
Faculty Revolt, and so on. Apparently any complete or sudden change in the conduct of human
affairs, with or without a violent confrontation or
an exchange of power, may properly be called a
revolution.

It is my thesis that the last three decades of the
twentieth century will witness a drastic change in
the business of providing instruction in schools
and colleges. Change by the year 2000 will be so
thoroughgoing that historians will have no difficulty
in agreeing that it was a revolution. You will note
the omission of words like "teaching" and "learning" in describing the coming revolution. Teaching
connotes for most of us an inherently person-medi-

ated activity and the vision of the "stand-up" lecturer comes most immediately to mind. One of the concomitants of the impending change is a major modification of the role of teacher. It is likely that future terms for teacher may be "instructional agent" or "lesson designer" or "instructional programmer." As for learning, we take the position that the word is not a way of describing an activity of the student, but rather a way of characterizing change in the student's behavior in some desired direction between two definite time markers. Pask[1] has pointed out that teaching is "excercising control of the instructional environment by arranging scope, sequence, materials, evaluation, and content for students." In other words, instruction is the general term for the process and learning is the product.

My objective is to challenge you with the shape of the instruction revolution, to point out how you as a teacher or administrator can cooperate and cope with it, and to suggest some of the social changes which are currently fueling this revolution.

At the secondary school level, American educators, beginning with Preston W. Search[2] in the late nineteenth century, have been interested in the goal of individualization. Between 1900 and 1930, disciples of Frederick Burk (see Brubacher[3] and Parkhurst[4]) devised and implemented several laboratory-type plans for self-instruction in the lower schools. These were self-pacing plans for the learner and demanded a great deal of versatility on the part of the teacher. Additional impetus for the theoretical interest of educators in individualization stemmed from the mental testing movement, beginning with the seminal work of Binet[5] about 60 years ago. Early intelligence

tests clearly showed differences in speed of task
completion among pupils, and these differences were
easily confirmed by a teacher's own observations of
mental agility. At the practical level, a great deal
of individualization took place in rural America's
one-room schools. Fifteen to 25 children spread un-
evenly through ages 6 to 14 necessarily committed
the teacher to large doses of individual pupil direction, recitation, and evaluation. With population
increases and school consolidations, most village
and rural schools began to look like rigidly graded
city schools. Teachers found themselves responsible
for larger and larger groups of children of approximately the same age and about the same physical
size. It is little wonder that some of the zest, enthusiasm, and obviousness of need for individualized
teaching was lost. When teachers complained about
too-large classes, the lack of time to spend with individual pupils, the wide diversity in pupil ability
level, many not-so-smart administrators introduced
"tracking" or "streaming" strategies. Separating
children into homogenous classes according to measured mental ability within age groups has been shown
conclusively to fail to increase the achievement
level of groups as a whole. [6] Homogeneous ability
grouping has, on the other hand, seriously exacer-
bated social problems connected with race and economic levels by "ghettoizing" classrooms within
the schools, even though the schools served racially
and economically mixed neighborhoods.

Whereas the common schools have some history of
experimentation with individualized instruction,
methods, higher education, led by the large state
universities, has pushed the development of mass
communication methods in instruction. The large

group lecture and the adaptation of closed-circuit television are examples of higher education's trend away from individualized instruction. Of course, the outstanding accomplishments of American university graduate schools could never have been achieved without the cost-savings introduced by mass communications techniques in their undergraduate colleges.

Interest in individualized instruction had a surge about 15 years ago when Harvard's B. F. Skinner[7, 8] advocated an education technology built around the use of rather crude teaching machines. It soon became apparent that there was no particular magic in the machines themselves, since they contained only short linear series of questions and answers to word problems called "frames." These programs were quickly put into book form and the programmed text was born. Although it enjoyed initial success, with some highly motivated learners, the programmed text has not caught on in either the lower schools or in higher education as a major instructional device. Industry and the military forces seem to have made the best use of programmed texts, perhaps because of a high degree of motivation on the part of many learners in those situations.

Most recently, an educational technique for the lower schools has been developed out of the work of the Learning Research and Development Center at the University of Pittsburgh. The method, called "individually prescribed instruction" or IPI, is development of a technology based on precise specification and delineation of educational objectives in behavioral terms. Pupils work individually on a precisely scaled set of materials with frequent interspersed diagnostic quizzes.

It must be clear, even after this sketchy review of
the history of individualized instruction, that the
concept has been pursued in a desultory fashion. I
have heard hour-long conversations on individualization by educators who have only the vaguest notion of what is encompassed by the concepts. Let me
review five different concepts of individualization
and acknowledge that I am indebted to Tyler[12] for
some of these distinctions.

First, most educators agree that instruction is
"individual" when the learner is allowed to proceed
through content materials at a self-determined pace
that is comfortable for him. This concept of self-
paced instruction is incorporated into all programmed
texts and is perhaps easiest to achieve with reading
material and hardest to achieve in a setting that
presents content by means of lectures, films, and
television. Octtinger,[13] in his witty but infuriating
little book, Run, Computer, Run refers to this self-
pacing concept of individualization as "rate tailoring."

A second concept of individualized instruction is that
the learner should be able to work at times convenient
to him. The hard realities of academic bookkeeping
with the associated paraphernalia of credits, marks,
and time-serving schedules make this concept difficult to implement in colleges or in the common schools.

That a learner should begin instruction in a given subject at a point appropriate to his past achievement is
a third way of looking at individualization. This concept
makes the assumption that progress in learning is linear and that the main task is to locate the learner's

present position on a universal continuum. Once properly located, he can then continue to the goal. These
notions seem to have their optimum validity for well-
ordered content like mathematics or foreign languages.
In fact, the advanced placement program which provides college credit for tested subject matter achievement during secondary school, is a gross attempt to
get at this kind of individualization.

A fourth concept of individualization is the idea that
learners are inhibited by a small number of easily
identifiable skills or knowledge. The assumption is
that the absence of these skills is diagnosable and that
remedial efforts through special instructional units
can eliminate the difficulty. Colleges and universities
seeking to enroll a higher proportion of their students
from among the culturally disadvantaged and the economically deprived will be forced to bring this concept
to bear if they wish to maintain current academic standards.

A fifth concept is that individualization can be achieved
by furnishing the learner with a wealth of instructional
media from which to choose. Lectures, audio tapes,
films, books, etc., all with the same intellectual content, could theoretically be made available to the
learner. The underlying notion is that the learner will
instinctively choose the communication medium or
combination of media that enable him to do his best
work. The research evidence to support this view-
point and practice is not at all strong. [14] Perhaps
even more persuasive than the lack of evidence is the
vanity of instructors who cannot understand why a
student would choose a film or an audio tape in preference to the instructor's own lively stimulating,
and informative lectures. [15]

I have reviewed five concepts of individualization
which have some credence in education, but by far
the most prevalent interpretation is the one of self-
pacing, or rate tailoring. These notions lead us
directly to the idea of adaptive education in responsive environments which I want to discuss shortly.
But first, one more distinction, "Individual instruction, " where one studies in isolation from other
learners, should probably be distinguished from
"individualized instructions, " where the scope, sequence, and time of instruction are tailored in one
or more of the five ways I have just described. "Individualized instruction" can still be in a group setting and, in fact, was commonly practiced in rural
one-room schools, as mentioned earlier. On the
other hand, "individual instruction" can be singular-
ly rigid, monotonous, and unresponsive to the needs
of the learner. You could, for instance, take programmed text material which is designed for individualized instruction and put it into an educational television format. Each frame could be shown to a
large group of students to pick a correct option and
then going on to another frame. This procedure
would be individual instruction with a vengeance.
But it forces a kind of lock-step on students of varying abilities and interests that is the antithesis
of "individualized instruction. "

ADAPTIVE EDUCATION

I predict that the impending instruction revolution
will shortly bypass the simple idea of individualizing
instruction and move ahead to the more sophisticated
notion of providing adaptive education for school and
college learners. By adaptive education we mean the
tailoring of subject matter presentations to fit the

special requirements and capabilities of each learner.
The ideal is that no learner should stop short of his
ultimate achievement in an area of content because of
idiosyncratic hang-ups in his particular study strategies.

We have seen how the concept of individualized instruction has been pretty well arrested at the level of encouraging the learner to vary and control his task completion time. Many additional, more psychologically
oriented variables will have to be brought into play
to achieve the goals of adaptive education, as well as
the adoption of individualizing techniques. We know a
great deal about individual differences among people
in regard to their sensory inputs, their reaction times,
their interests, their values and preferences, and their
organizational strategies in "mapping" the cognitive
world. What we do not know very much about is the extent to which, or how, these easily tested, individual
difference variables affect the acquisition and retention of new knowledge. Psychological learning theory
has been pre-occupied with the study of variables in
extremely simple stimulus-response situations, and
investigations of meaningful learning phenomena have
clearly dealt with human subjects as if they were all
cut from the same bolt. The exception to this observation is, of course, the variable of measured mental ability, which has been shown to be related to
achievement in conventionally presented instruction and
has been carefully controlled in many learning experiments involving human subjects.

Essential to the idea of adaptive education is the means
of utilizing new knowledge about individual differences
among learners to bring a highly tailored instructional
product to the student. As long as we are dealing with

static or canned linear presentations such as those
contained in books, films, video tapes, and some lectures, there seems to be little incentive to try to discover what modifications in instructional materials
would optimize learning for each student. To plug
this important gap in the drive toward vastly im-
proved learning, the modern digital computer seems
to have great promise. About a decade ago, Rath,
Anderson and Brainerd. [16] suggested the application
of the computer to teaching tasks and actually programmed some associative learning material. In the
intervening decade, a number of major universities,
medical schools, industries, and military establish-
ments have been exploring the use of the computer
in instruction. Five years ago we instituted a computer-assisted instruction laboratory at Penn State
and have been trying to perfect new instructional
techniques within the constraints of available hardware and computer operating systems. [17, 18, 19, 20]
There are, according to my estimates, some 35 to
40 active computer-assisted instruction (CAI) installations operating in the world today, and fewer
than 100 completed semester-length courses or their
equivalent. Almost none of these courses have been
constructed according to the ideals I mentioned for
adaptive education. Indeed, many of them look like
crude, made-over versions of programmed textbooks, but this does not disturb me when I recall
that the earliest automobiles were designed to look
like carriages without the horses. The fact is that
the modern computer's information storage capacity
and decision logic have given us a glimpse of what
a dynamic, individualized instruction procedure
could be, and some insight into how this tool might
be brought to bear to achieve an adaptive quality
education for every student. We do not claim that

the achievement of this goal is just around the corner
or that every school and college can implement it by
the turn of the century. We do believe that progress
toward a program of adaptive education will be the big
difference between our best schools and our mediocre
ones at the end of the next three decades.

What individual different variables look most promising
for adapting instruction to the individual student via
CAI? At Penn State we are testing the idea that a person learns best if he is rewarded for correctness
with his most preferred type of reinforcement.[21] Thus
some students will, we believe, learn more rapidly
if they receive encouragement in the form of adult
approval. Others will perform better if they receive
actual tokens for excellence at significant places in
the program, the tokens being exchangeable for candy,
cokes, or other wanted objects. Still others respond
to competitive situations in which they are given evidence of the superiority or inferiority of their performance compared to that of their peers. It is a fairly
simple matter to determine a learner's reward preference in advance of instruction and to provide him
with a computer-based program in which the information feedback is tailored to his psychological preference.

Perhaps the most dynamic and relevant variable on
which to base an adaptive program of instruction is
the learner's immediate past history of responses.
By programming the computer to count and evaluate
the correctness of the 10 most recent responses it
is possible to determine what comes next for each
learner accordind go a prearranged schedule. For
example, four or fewer correct out of the most recent 10 might dictate branching into shorter teaching

steps with heavy prompting and large amounts of practice material. A score of five to seven might indicate
the need for just a little more practice material, and
eight or more correct out of the 10 most recent problems would suggest movement into a fast "track" with
long strides through the computer-presented content.
The dynamic part of this adaptive mechanism is that
the computer constantly updates its performance information about each learner by dropping off the
learner's response to the tenth problem back as it
adds on new performance information from a just-
completed problem.

There are two rather distinct strategies for present-
ing subject matter to learners. One is deductive, in
which a rule, principle, or generalization is presented, followed by examples. The other strategy is
inductive and seeks, by means of a careful choice of
illustrative examples, to lead the learner into formulating principles and generalizations on his own init-
iative. In the lower schools, inductive method is
called "guided discovery" and has been found useful
by many teachers. Our belief at the Penn State CAI
laboratory is that these two presentation strategies
have their corollaries in an individual differences
variable and that, for some students, learning will
be facilitated by the deductive approach; others will
learn more rapidly and with better retention if an
inductive mode is adopted. A strong program of adaptive education would take these and other identifiable
learner variables into account in the instructional
process.

EVALUATION AND STUDENT APPRAISAL

One of the important concomitants of the instruction
revolution will be a drastic revision in the approach

to learner evaluation and grading practices by faculty.
Even the moderate students on campus are saying that
letter grades are anachronistic. On many campuses,
including our own, students have petitioned for, and
won, the right to receive "satisfactory" and "unsatisfactory" evaluations of their work in certain non-ma-
jor courses. Other students have attacked all grades
as a manifestation of a coercive, competitive, ma-
terialistic society. Without admitting to being a tool
of a sick society, we should change this part of the
business of higher education as rapidly as possible.

It seems to me that most formal instruction has been
predicated on the notion that a course is offered between two relatively fixed points in time. In addition,
the tools of instruction, such as lectures, textbooks,
references, and computer services, are all relatively
fixed and are the same for all learners. To be sure,
the students do vary the amount of time they spend
with these tools. Even there, the college catalogue
tells the students that they should all study three hours
outside of class for every hour in class. At the close
of the period of instruction or end of the course, usually the end of the term, we give the students an achievement test that is constructed in a way that will maximize the differences among their scores. To get this
seemingly important differentiation between our students in achievement , we have to ask extremely difficult questions. Sometimes we even go so far as
to ask questions about footnotes in the text. In fact,
we often have to ask questions on topics or objectives
that we have made no attempt to teach. Our rationalization for this tactic is that we want the students
to be able to transfer their knowledge. After obtaining the achievement examination results, we consult
the trusty "normal curve" and assign A's, B's, C's,

D's, and F's according to our interpretation of the
grading mores of the institution. With time and materials fixed, we are essentially capitalizing upon
the same human abilities. that are measured by
intelligence tests. Thus it is not surprising that intelligence and teacher-assigned grades tend to be
highly correlated.

We could, as collegiate educators, do society and
ourselves a big favor by making a fundamental shift
in our approach to teaching and examining. (Incidentally, we might generate some relevance "points"
with our students.) First, we should say (and mean)
that our job is helping each of our students to
achieve mastery over some operationally defined
portion of subject matter. [22] Furthermore, failure
by any student putting forth an effort is a failure on
our part as teachers, or a breakdown of the selection system. Now, to do this job we will have to get
rid of a lot of the present practices and irrelevancies
of higher education. There is no point in maintaining
an adversary system in the classroom, with the students against the instructor and each of the students
against each other. Society may think that it wants
us to mark our students on a competitive scale, but
how much more sensible it would be if we could say,
on the basis of accumulated examination evidence,
that John Jones has achieved 85 percent of the objectives in Engineering 101, rather than to say that
he got a "B. " If our job is to help the student master the subject matter or come close--say, achieve
90 percent or greater of the objectives--then we are
going to have to adapt our instruction to him. As a
starter, we could individualize by letting the student
pace his own instruction. We know, for example,
from preliminary work with class-sized groups in
computer-assisted instruction, that the slowest stu-

dent will take from three to five times as long as the fastest student in a rich environment of individualized teaching material. During a recent computer-mediated in-service teacher education course presented by Penn State in Dryden, Virginia, to 129 elementary school teachers, the average completion time was 21 clock hours. The fastest student finished in 12 hours and the slowest took 58 hours. [23]

Student evaluations should also be based on the concept that an achievable mastery criterion exists for each course. We should no longer engage in the sophistry of classical psychometrics, in which we prepare a test or examination deliberately designed to make half the students get half the items wrong. It is true that such a test optimally discriminates among the learners, which we justify by claiming need for competitive marking information. If however, 50 percent of the students get 50 percent of the answers wrong, then either we are asking the wrong questions or there is something seriously wrong with our nonadaptable instructional program.

Under optimum circumstances, we might get an enlightened view of the faculty's need to adopt mastery of student evaluation procedures and might get professors to talk less, but we would still be faced with the psychological problem of instructor dominance or instructor power. The power over students which the "giving" of grades confers on professors would not be yielded easily by many in college teaching today. As Pogo says, "I have met the enemy and he is us."

If we, as faculty and administrators in higher education, embraced the notion of teaching for student mastery, and means of individually adaptive programs, then these are some of the concomitants:

1. Instructors would have to state their course objectives in behavioral terms.
2. Achievement tests keyed to course objectives would have to be constructed and used as both diagnostic placement and end-of-course determiners.
3. The bachelor's degree might take from two to eight years instead of the traditional four, because of the wide-variability in mastery achievement.
4. Instead of telling three times a week, instructors might have to spend their time listening to students individually and in small groups where progress toward subject mastery required careful monitoring.
5. Instead of being primarily concerned with a discipline or with a specialization, those who profess for undergraduates would have to make the student and his knowledge their first concern.
6. Evaluation for promotion and salary increments for college teachers would be based on measured amounts of growth exhibited by their students and on numbers of students who achieved a specific mastery criterion.

If professors and deans ignore the reasoned demands for reform of undergraduate instruction which come from the students, the government, and a concerned citizenry, then the revolution will be ugly and wrenching. The so-called "free universities," with their obvious shortcomings, are already harbingers of the chaos into which traditional higher education could slip if there is no responsiveness on the part of a majority of academicians to the need for change.

In the current wave of student unrest, many of the best articulated issues are local in nature, like the quality of food in the cafeteria or the relaxation of dormitory visiting rules for members of the opposite sex. Underneath these surface issues, however, lies the one big issue, which the students themselves haven't spelled out clearly. This is the issue of the relevance of contemporary collegiate instruction for students' lives. It seems to me students are saying, albeit not very clearly, that they want some wise adult to care about them, to pay attention to them, to listen and to guide them. We sit on our status quo's and ignore their cry for help at our peril.

INCREASING HETEROGENEITY

Part of the fuel breeding the revolution in instruction is the increasing heterogeneity in mental ability and scholastic preparation among college students. The combined power of the teaching faculty, regional accrediting agencies, and shortage of spaces for students, has until recently, enabled many public universities to become increasingly selective. In fact, prestige among higher education institutions has been closely correlated with the height of the norms for entrance test scores. Even the great state universities, which began under the land-grant aegis as people's colleges, have a kind of "elitest" aura about them. Rising aspirations of minority groups, particularly blacks, have pointed up the fact that the poor, the disadvantaged, and the dark-skinned of our society do not share equally in whatever benefits a post-secondary college experience confers. A recent study and report by John Egerton for the National Association of State Universities and Land-Grant Colleges[24] was based on 80 public universities which enroll almost one-third of the nation's college students. He found that less than two percent of the graduate and undergraduate students were Negro in

these institutions and that less than one percent of
the faculty were black. Yet approximately 11 percent
of the total U.S. population is black. It seems irrefutable that, with society's new awareness of the in-
equality in higher education, university entrance standards will have to be lowered for sizeable groups of
blacks who have been   poorly educated in the nation's
secondary schools. Accounts of City University of
New York's open admissions plan for fall, 1970,
provide ample proof of the beginning of this trend,
and Healy's[25] recent article firms up the humani-
tarian and social theory for the change in this great
university. The lowering of entrance requirements
will inevitably increase the heterogeneity of scholastic skills which makes the conventional teaching job
so difficult.

Another source for increasing individual differences
among college undergraduates is their stiffening resistance to required courses. Students clearly want
more freedom of choice in devising their éducation
programs. They want to determine what subjects are
relevant to their lives and are increasingly impatient
with elaborate prerequisites and multi-course se-
quences. Although the activists are not likely to win
a complete victory on this score, the pressure which
they generate will serve to breach the walls and
gates around courses that have carefully been built
by faculty over the years in order to make the conventional job of teaching somewhat more manageable.
In addition to the student rejection of required courses,
there is a corresponding need for the teaching
of interdisciplinary subjects. Students see, perhaps
more clearly than the faculty, that solution of the
nation's problems, such as urban decay, congestion,
air and water pollution, and war and peace are not

going to be solved by the unitary application of knowledge from traditional disciplines. For purposes of
this discussion, the drive toward more interdisciplinary courses of study can only increase the heterogeneity among students which the faculty has labored
to minimize.

CONCLUSION

I have argued that we are now living with the early
stages of a revolution in instruction which will be
more or less complete by the turn of the century. The
major changes will be primarily characterized by
individualization of instruction leading to sophisticated
systems of adaptive education. Two concomitants
of the revolution which seriously concern college faculty and administrators are the need for new fundamental concepts of student appraisal and adaptation to
increasing heterogeneity among the students in our
charge.

Mr. Mitzel (1368, Pennsylvania State University
Chapter) is professor of educational psychology,
Pennsylvania State University. This article is a
slightly revised and shortened version of a paper
he presented at an annual meeting of the American
Society for Engineering Education, held at University
Park, Pa., in June, 1969. The complete paper appears
in the Journal of the American Society for Engineering
Education for March, 1970.

Notes and References

1. G. Pask, "Computer-Assisted Learning and Teaching," paper presented at Seminar on Computer–Based Learning. Leeds University, September, 1969.
2. P. W. Search, "Individual Teaching: The Pueblo Plan. " Education Review, February, 1894.
3. J. S. Brubacher, A History of the Problems of Education, 2nd ed, New York: McGraw-Hill, 1966.
4. H. H. Parkhurst, Education of the Dalton Plan, New York: E. P. Dutton & Co. 1922.
5. A. Binet and T. Simon. The Development of Intelligence in Children, trans. Elizabeth S. Kits. Vineland, N. J. : The Training School, 1916.
6. J. I. Goodlad in Encyclopedia of Educational Research 3rd ed. , ed. C. Harris New York Macmillan, 1960.
7. B. F. Skinner, "Teaching Machines, " Science, 1958.
8. B. F. Skinner, "The Science of Learning and the Art of Teaching, "Harvard Educational Review, Spring, 1954.
9. C. M. Lindvall and J. O.Bolvin, " Programmed Instruction in the Schools:An Application of Programming Principles in Individually Prescribed Instruction," in Programmed Instruction, ed. P. C. Lange. Chicago: The University of Chicago Press, 1967.
10. R. Glaser, The Education of Individuals, Pittsburgh, Pa. : Learning Research and Development Center, University of Pittsburgh, 1966.
11. W. W. Cooley and R. Glaser, "An Information Management System for Individually Prescribed Instruction, " working paper No. 44, Learning Research and Development Center, University of Pittsburgh, mimeographed, 1968.
12. R. W. Tyler, "New Directions in Individualizing Instruction, " in The Abington Conference '67 on New Directions in Individualizing Instruction, Abington, Pa.

Notes and References (cont'd)

13. A. G. Oettinger and S. Marks, Run, Computer, Run. Cambridge, Mass, :Harvard University Press, 1969.

14. N. Postiethwait, "Planning for Better Learning, " in In Search of Leaders, ed. G. K. Smith, Washington, D. C. : American Association for Higher Education, NEA, 1967.

15. D. T. Tosti and J. T. Ball, A Behaviorial Approach to Instructional Design and Media Selection, BSD Paper No. 1. Observations in Behavioral Technology Albuquerque, N. M. : The Behavior Systems Division Westinghouse Learning Corporation, 1969.

16. G. J. Rath, N. S. Anderson, and R. C. Brainerd, "The IBM Research Center Teaching Machine Project, " In Automatic Teaching: The State of the Art, ed. E. H. Galanter, New York: Wiley, 1959.

17. H. E. Mitzel. The Development and Presentation of Four College Courses by Computer Teleprocessing. Final Report, Computer-Assisted Instruction Laboratory, The Pennsylvania State University, June 30, 1967. Contract No. OE-4-16010 New Project No. 5-1194. US Office of Education.

18. H. E. Mitzel, B. R. Brown, and R. Igo. The Development and Evaluation of a Teleprocessed Computer-Assisted Instruction Course in the Recognition of Malarial Parasites. Final Report No. R-17, Computer-Assisted Instruction Laboratory, The Pennsylvania State University, June 30, 1968. Contract No. N00014-67-A-0385-0003, Office of Naval Research.

19. H. E. Mitzel, Experimentation with Computer-Assisted Instruction in Technical Education, Semiannual progress report, R-18, Computer-Assisted Instruction Laboratory, The Pennsylvania State University, December 31, 1968.

Notes and References (cont'd)

20. "Inquiry, " Research Report published by the
    Office of the Vice President for Research, Penn
    State.
21. C. A. Cartwright and G. P. Cartwright, Reward
    Preference Profiles of Elementary School
    Children, mimeographed. Computer-Assited
    Instruction Laboratory. The Pennsylvania
    State University, 1969. Paper presented at
    the meeting of the American Educational Research
    Association, Los Angeles, February, 1969.
22. B. Bloom, "Learning for Mastery, " UCLA
    Evaluation Comment, 1968.
23. K. H. Hall, et al. , Inservice Mathematics
    Education for Elementary School Teachers via
    Computer-Assisted Instruction. Interim Report,
    No. R-19. Computer-Assisted Instruction. Labor-
    atory, The Pennsylvania State University, June
    1, 1969.
24. B. Nelson, "State Universities: Report Terms
    Desegregation "Largely Token, " Science, June
    6, 1969.
25. T. S. Healy, "Will Everyman Destroy the
    University? " Saturday Review, December, 1969.